9106

Blairsville-Saltsburg Schools

EDEA II
1975

SINCLAIR LEWIS

Modern Literature Monographs

SINCLAIR LEWIS

James Lundquist

ESEAH
1975

813
LUN

Frederick Ungar Publishing Co.
New York

Second Printing, 1975

Contents

Chronology

1885: Harry Sinclair Lewis is born on 7 February in Sauk Centre, Minnesota.

1902: Enters Oberlin Academy in Ohio in preparation for Yale University.

1903: Enrolls at Yale.

1906: Leaves Yale for Upton Sinclair's colony at Helicon Hall, Englewood, New Jersey. Later lives in New York as a free-lance writer and editor.

1908: Graduates from Yale.

1908–1915: Travels across the United States and holds a variety of editorial jobs.

1912: Publishes first novel, *Hike and the Aeroplane,* under the pseudonym of Tom Graham.

1914: Marries Grace Hegger in New York. *Our Mr. Wrenn* is published.

1915: *Trail of the Hawk* is published. Lewis becomes a full-time writer.

1916: Drives from Sauk Centre to Seattle in a Ford.

1917: *The Job* and *The Innocents* are published. A son, Wells Lewis, is born.

1919: *Free Air* is published.

1920: *Main Street* is published.

1922: *Babbitt* is published. Lewis makes intermittent trips to Europe throughout the 1920s.

1925: *Arrowsmith* is published.

1926: *Mantrap* is published. Lewis refuses the Pulitzer Prize for *Arrowsmith*. His father dies.

1927: *Elmer Gantry* is published.

1928: *The Man Who Knew Coolidge* is published. Lewis is divorced from Grace. Marries Dorothy Thompson in England. Buys farm at Barnard, Vermont.

1929: *Dodsworth* is published.

1930: Receives a Nobel Prize. A son, Michael is born.

1933: *Ann Vickers* is published.

1934: *Work of Art* is published. Works on dramatization of *Dodsworth* and collaborates with Lloyd Lewis on *Jayhawker,* which is produced in New York.

1935: *Selected Short Stories* and *It Can't Happen Here* are published. Becomes a member of the National Institute of Arts and Letters.

1936: Yale awards Lewis an honorary degree.

1938: *The Prodigal Parents* is published. Writes "Book Week" column for *Newsweek*. Performs as an actor and works as a playwright, producer, and director off and on during the 1930s.

1940: *Bethel Merriday* is published. Teaches writing at the University of Wisconsin.

1942: Lewis is divorced from Dorothy Thompson. Teaches writing at the University of Minnesota.

1943: *Gideon Planish* is published.

1944: Wells Lewis is killed in action.

1945: Buys a house in Duluth, Minnesota. *Cass Timberlane* is published.

1946: Moves to and later buys Thorvale Farm in Massachusetts.

1947: *Kingsblood Royal* is published.

1949: *The God-Seeker* is published. Travels to Italy.

1951: Lewis dies 10 January of heart disease in Rome. His ashes are buried in Sauk Centre. *World So Wide* is published.

1

The Exaggerated
Melodrama

We do know that almost from the beginnings of American writing the best documentors of the native scene have fought the battle of the lonely and the hunted.

—Jean Shepherd, Introduction to
The America of George Ade

Sinclair Lewis "was lean and tough looking as a long string of jerked beef and he had long talon-ended pale hands and a high doming forehead and quick though cracked lips and swift eyes that seemed to notice everything."[1] This is an image of a man whose life could be redeemed only by his toughness, his ability to endure critical and personal attacks of the sort few writers have ever suffered. And it is an image of a man who tried to see things as they were—the small town, the businessman, the scientist, the preacher, the demagogue, the philanthropist, the judge, and later but not too late, even himself.

On the surface, the career of Sinclair Lewis seems suggestive of so much in United States culture that Mark Schorer was prompted to subtitle his biography of him "An American Life." His story is, after all, an archetypal one: a bookish misfit grows up in an obscure country town in the middle of the continent, demands and gets an education in an eastern university, struggles through a painful apprenticeship as a writer, hits it big on a series of shocking best-selling novels, and then drinks himself to death through long years of decline. The only thing wrong with this story is that it is not true; the melodrama of Sinclair Lewis's life has been greatly exaggerated.

Harry Sinclair Lewis was born on 7 February 1885 in the little town he was later to make famous, Sauk Centre, Minnesota, then as now a town of a few thousand inhabitants, about one hundred miles northwest of

Minneapolis. He was the youngest son in a family of three boys. His father, Edwin J. Lewis, was a tight-lipped country doctor, a man who built up a sizeable fortune and a good reputation through hard work; and like most hard workers he was a man with a schedule. Even after Sinclair Lewis had become an established writer, visits back home meant submission once again to Dr. Lewis's regimen of breakfast at six-thirty, dinner at noon, and supper at six sharp.

Dr. Lewis was a man who liked to have things done his way, and he has often been portrayed as the model of the domineering Victorian father. But he was less than harsh on his sons. Young Harry (Sinclair went by his baptismal name until he became a writer) had plenty of time to read, indulge his fancy, and take part in the traditional sports of the country boy. He never was forced to do any work, outside of household chores, cutting grass, and chopping wood. Even when he went against his father's wishes by insisting on college in the east instead of at the University of Minnesota, Dr. Lewis gave in to him. The shadow Dr. Lewis cast over his best-known son's life was not without its benefits: Sinclair Lewis's writing habits were the very model of his father's notion of hard work—an early breakfast, writing until dinner, perhaps a nap, more work, a walk, supper, entertainment of some sort in the evening, and then early to bed. When he was not writing, his life was chaotic, but when he had a novel going, not even his father could have faulted his method. "With the tools of his work he was as scrupulous as his father was with his surgical instruments," Vincent Sheean testified. "Sharpened pencils, notebooks, paper, carbon were always in the same place. His writing table was never littered, and what he had written was neatly stacked each day."[2]

One might think that the ingredients for tragedy

in Sinclair Lewis's life might be found in the death of his mother when he was six years old. But Mrs. Lewis had been sick with tuberculosis so much of the time after Harry's birth that he did not know her well enough to experience any great sense of loss at her death. He mentions her only seldom in his writing, probably because his stepmother, Isabel Warner, whom Dr. Lewis married a little over a year after his first wife's death, was such a good mother to him. The second Mrs. Lewis was, by Sauk Centre standards, a cultured woman. She came from Chicago, was interested in literature and music, and soon became a dominant figure in Sauk Centre women's clubs. More important, she was sympathetic to Harry, took him with her on trips back to Chicago, and respected his early bookishness.

The nearest thing to trauma—and it hardly can be called that—in Sinclair Lewis's boyhood was his relationship with his brothers, particularly with Claude, the middle son, who was six years older than Harry and good in all the things that gave Harry problems—hunting, fishing, swimming, and managing his own life. Claude went to medical school and became a successful surgeon in Saint Cloud, a city of forty thousand some forty miles east of Sauk Centre. Harry wanted to compete with Claude, but very early on he realized that there was no way in which he could: he did not give athletics a serious try, he did more reading than hunting, and he decided against venturing his fortunes in medical school, even though that is what Dr. Lewis would have liked. Instead of intense rivalry developing between Harry and Claude, a pattern of honest respect resulted, at least insofar as Harry was concerned. Sinclair Lewis the writer consistently spoke of Claude with great admiration. Throughout his adult life Lewis maintained contact with Claude and Claude's family, and Claude in turn had an older brother's concerned affection for Harry. Fred, the oldest of the Lewis boys, seems to figure not at all in the development of his youngest brother. Ten years older than Harry, Fred was not much of a success at anything and lived a quiet small-town life.

The larger setting for Sinclair Lewis's boyhood, the town of Sauk Centre, is often thought of as the typical turn-of-the-century midwestern town, a place in which the people were repressed by grim religion and depressed by a desolate collection of false-front buildings set in the midst of endless cornfields. It is not that way now, nor was it that way in the late-nineteenth century when Harry Lewis was growing up there. Sauk Centre is about as far west as you can get without quite being western, and it is about as far north as you can get without being in the north woods. It but little resembles in appearance and atmosphere an Illinois, Indiana, Iowa, or Ohio small town. The land around Sauk Centre is rolling prairie broken by extensive woodlots, not really prime farm country. Lakes are everywhere, the town itself fronting two sides of Sauk Lake. Just a few miles to the north, around the town of Alexandria, the part of Minnesota described as "Vacationland" begins and continues up to the Canadian border.

As the visitor to Sauk Centre is usually surprised to find out, the town that Lewis used as the model for Gopher Prairie in *Main Street* is a very pleasant place indeed, one of the most attractive small towns in the United States. The deadly aura of freshwater religion that Lewis's good friend H. L. Mencken so often attacked never hung over Sauk Centre, mainly because no single church ever became dominant in the town; Lutherans, Catholics, Episcopalians, Baptists, and Congregationalists have all had to be satisfied with simply getting along together in Sauk Centre. And Harry Lewis's parents were not at all forceful in prescribing a religious affiliation for him, although young Harry went willingly to Sunday school and church.

Sauk Centre was not Friendship Village and Harry Lewis did not grow up without his fair share of uncertainty, humiliation, and rejection; but he certainly was not devastated by anything that happened to him as a gangling, unathletic, and plain-looking youth. His admiration for Claude and his eagerness to tag along with Claude's friends on expeditions into the countryside often left him in the position of pest, and many times he was the victim, as younger boys usually are, of the older boys' practical jokes—the clothes tied in knots during the swimming trip, the "ditchings" in the woods, the games in which the least-knowing boy is duped into being the perpetual "it." But Harry tagged along anyway—when he was not reading.

In talking to an interviewer, the old people in Sauk Centre who grew up with Sinclair Lewis will inevitably mention that "Harry Lewis must've read, one way or another, darned near all the books in the Bryant Library." He may not have read all the books, but he most certainly worked his way through the fiction shelves reading the works of Scott, Dickens, Kipling (the three novelists, along with H. G. Wells, who seem to have influenced his later style the most), Thackeray, Tolstoy, and Hugo, as well as the poetry of Longfellow and Tennyson. This reading is often seen as evidence of Harry's withdrawal from his Sauk Centre surroundings, and to some extent much of the reading he did was escape reading—which is to say that he read for the same reason that most boys who are inclined toward books do. One should be careful about seeing too much in Harry Lewis's devotion to the library; that he simply liked to read (and read extensively throughout his life) is a much better explanation for it than that he was retreating from a hostile environment.

Harry did not have many close friends as a child, but by the time he was in high school he was far from being the loner bookish boys sometimes become. His high-school diaries repeatedly mention his "hell raising," his teasing of the freshmen girls, his illegal experimenting in the chemistry lab, his late hours (staying out past eleven). He was president of the freshman and sophomore literary society and active in debating; he delivered the oration at a Thanksgiving program, and he had the lead in the senior-class play. In addition he wrote the class motto and was the author of most of the class cheers. He was not an athlete and he did not have a steady girl, but he was an important and, in many ways, respected member of the class of 1902. And when he returned from Yale to Sauk Centre in 1905 for his summer vacation, he was welcomed back by his high-school classmates as something of a man of the world.

He was anything but a man of the world when he enrolled at Yale in the fall of 1903 after a year of preparatory work at Oberlin College in Ohio. By the time he graduated, however, he was sophisticated intellectually, if not socially, above the level of his fellow students. The transformation that took place during his college years was due to the same fiery energy that made the nickname "Red" so appropriate. He was an erratic but good student and when he worked he worked hard. When he was not studying or writing stories, poems, and articles for the Yale literary magazine, *The Lit,* he was exploring New Haven, Boston, and New York. During two summer vacations he worked his way to England on cattle boats, and in the fall of his senior year he dropped out of school to work as a janitor in Upton Sinclair's socialist colony at Helicon Hall, Englewood,

New Jersey. He stayed out of school the rest of that academic year to try to make it as a free-lance writer, to work on the editorial staff of the magazine *Transatlantic Tales,* and to travel to the Canal Zone to find a construction job or any job he could get (but he got none). By the time he graduated in 1908 (his name was listed with the class of 1907), he had been an editor of *The Lit,* had been successful enough as a student to have been encouraged to take a Ph.D. in English, and had traveled on his own halfway around the world from Sauk Centre. He was somewhat bohemian in appearance and more than somewhat determined to do one thing: write.

The next twelve years of Lewis's life were, by all indications, his happiest. These years were a time of travel and development through a series of jobs and interludes between jobs, a time in which he moved toward a discovery of the style and subject matter that were to become distinctly his own. After leaving New Haven and returning to Sauk Centre for a few weeks after graduation, Lewis took a job as editorial writer, reporter, drama critic, and nearly everything else except paper boy for the Waterloo, Iowa, *Courier*. He lasted ten weeks before he caught a train to New York, where he worked as a night clerk for a charity organization (an experience he capitalized on in his 1943 exposé of philanthropy, *Gideon Planish*). His first important work accepted for publication was a story called "They That Take the Sword." *Red Book Magazine* paid him seventy-five dollars to publish the story, and this gave him the confidence to quit his charity job and take off for the writers' and painters' colony at Carmel, California.

Lewis's Carmel experience—living in a shack with William Rose Benét, drinking muscatel, eating abalone, tramping along the beach, going to artists' parties, pretending to work as a secretary for another writer (Grace Macgowan Cook), and all the while trying to get stories, poetry, and articles down on paper—was the kind of life that most would-be writers dream about when they sit in their rooms and think of what ought to be. It was not a productive period, but it gave Lewis a taste of the independent life that he struggled through the next few years, one might say through the rest of his life, to regain but never quite did.

After Carmel he worked for the San Francisco *Evening Bulletin* as a reporter, the Associated Press as a wire editor, *Sunset* magazine as a roaming correspondent (within California), and for Jack London as a plot writer. Then he headed back east, where he went through a series of editorial jobs with the *Volta Review* (a magazine for the deaf), Frederick A. Stokes Publishing Company, *Adventure* magazine, the Publishers' Newspaper Syndicate (as editor of a nationally distributed book-review section), and the George H. Doran Company. He was a good editor and would probably have had a career in the publishing business had he not, by the end of 1915, established himself well enough as a writer to risk all with his typewriter and resign from his job with Doran. He had gotten his short stories into many magazines, including *The Saturday Evening Post,* and he had published his first novels, *Hike and the Aeroplane* (a boys' book written under the pseudonym of Tom Graham) in 1912, *Our Mr. Wrenn* in 1914, and *The Trail of the Hawk* in 1915. Readers are sometimes surprised to learn that Lewis published three more novels—*The Job,* 1917; *The Innocents,* 1917; and *Free Air,* 1919—before he finally established his reputation with *Main Street* in 1920. His development was slow and, at times, unpromising, but Lewis went at it with an amount of drive that can only be respected. His period of apprenticeship was not a time of romantic agony; it was a time of hard work, eased considerably by the personal happiness and emotional stability that followed his marriage to Grace Hegger in 1914.

Lewis was not quite an Anthony Trollope in his attitude toward writing; that is, he did not work with his watch beside him on the desk and go about his labors as if he were a clerk or businessman. But in the years preceding *Main Street,* Lewis came up with an approach to writing that seemed to combine the disciplines of newspaper reporter, editorial writer, beachcomber, magazine editor, and publisher's assistant. He gathered material wherever he could find it, sorted it out and reflected on it, always looking for the story that would please and disturb his readers at the same time; and he kept a sharp eye out for something that would sell. Lewis was searching for a way of writing that would pull readers to him and that would also pull him out of the obscurity—one could not call it poverty—he struggled against upon his graduation from Yale.

The style he came up with can be seen in its development as a movement back toward the linguistic patterns of his native Minnesota. *Hike and the Aeroplane* is hack work, written, as Lewis frankly admitted, to give him money with which to buy time for the writing of *Our Mr. Wrenn.* Lewis's second novel reads (as virtually every commentator on it has remarked) like H. G. Wells, whom Lewis did attempt to imitate. *Our Mr. Wrenn* is similar to Wells's *Mr. Polly* and is a pleasant, and in many ways, graceful story about the little man, in Lewis's case a clerk, who longs for a fuller life, tries to find it when a small fortune falls his way, and then turns to the security and restrained pleasure of a wife and home. *The Trail of the Hawk* is not quite as derivative as *Our Mr. Wrenn,* but it is the kind of novel Jack London could have written. Carl (Hawk) Ericson, a small-town boy with mechanical aptitude and a taste for adventure, makes his mark as an aviator and then becomes a businessman-adventurer, developing the "Touricar," an automobile camper (one of several business ideas Lewis had had that subsequently proved profitable, though not to him).

The Job, a muckraking treament of a woman's attempt to succeed in the man's world of business, has the flavor of Upton Sinclair and Theodore Dreiser. Because of its defense of feminism and its acknowledgment of sexual conflict, it was the first Lewis novel to cause a stir. The novel can be seen as Lewis's version of the *Sister Carrie* story. *The Innocents,* published the same year as *The Job,* revealed the inconsistency that troubled Lewis throughout his creative life. It is a silly tale about an old couple who find themselves suddenly out of money and prospects; but they are cheerful enough about it even though they are forced to take to the road. Along the way they find friendly derelicts whom they befriend and inspire through their own joviality. They get to Indiana, are welcomed in a small town, and find both employment and happiness in managing a shoe store.

In its quietness and in its genial defense of the inherent goodness of the American middle west, *The Innocents* does give voice to the longing for normalcy that arose in the United States during World War I—evidence that Lewis was developing the sensitivity to the moods of his countrymen that was to serve him so well during the next decade. Actually, however, it serves as an example of how Lewis could, again and again, follow a good book with another that is not only bad but that does not even read as if it were written by the same author. An explanation for this could be found in Lewis's erratic personality, but perhaps a better one is that he wrote too

much and that he wrote some books when he should not
have been writing anything. *The Innocents* reads as if it
were written by a tired writer—as do the later "bad"
novels *Mantrap, Work of Art,* and *The God-Seeker.*

But with *Free Air,* Lewis was back on the track.
The beginning of the novel is set in Minnesota. The central character, Milt Daggett, a Minnesota garage me-
chanic, decides on a cross-country pursuit of the vaca-
tioning Claire Boltwood, with whom he has fallen in
love. Much of the novel's documentation came from a
Sauk-Centre-to-Seattle automobile trip Lewis and his
wife had made in 1916. The Lewis style that was to become familiar to most readers with *Main Street* a year
later first became distinct in *Free Air.* The ear for slang
and for Minnesota talk is there, along with the practice
of using the device of cataloging in describing characters, landscapes, buildings, rooms, and nearly anything
needing description. The ragtime and ricky-ticky rhythms
of 1920s America are there, the rhythms of a writer who
grew up writing for the popular, instead of the under-
ground, magazines. All the slickness, all the garishness,
all the loudness of which Lewis was later accused—it is
all there. But the ability to conceive characters who rep-
resent, in an uncanny way, American types; to have
them talk a language of brand names; and to have them
ironically believe, no matter what happens, in the bucolic philosophy of happiness through love in the world's
only democracy and fairest land—all this is the essential
Lewis and it is also to be found in *Free Air.*

One aspect of *Free Air* that ought to be discussed
by itself is Lewis's point of view, which has been seen by
many readers of his later novels as contradictory or, at
best, ambiguous. Side by side in *Free Air* and in all of
Lewis's novels that have Minnesota-like settings, are his
love of place and people and his satirical attacks on the

same places and the same people. On the one hand is "the sweep and exhilaration of the great open country" that impressed a reviewer in the *New Republic*.[3] On the other hand, the novel is, in several places, a testament to what one critic called Lewis's "malevolent and uncharitable eye and ear."[4] The country is beautiful, the townspeople are often friendly and charming; but the country is also hard and desolate, the people are often conceited bumpkins, and the small towns always have grubby hotels with high-sounding names. What Lewis did was to play one set of values off against another in the classic practice of the satirist, but he gave it an additional twist.

The sets of values in *Free Air* are the eastern opinions of Mr. Boltwood, who is from Brooklyn Heights, New York, and the western attitudes of Milt; this is, of course, a traditional conflict in American culture. The Boltwoods are intelligent and sophisticated, but they are not self-sufficient on the prairie. Milt is uncouth, but he knows how to read a map and repair engines. Lewis does not use Milt to devastate the worth of the Boltwoods' opinions and way of life; nor does he use the Boltwoods to make Milt look like a hopeless provincial. By playing both sets of values against each other, Lewis achieved a benign kind of satire that cuts both ways but does not cut all the way through. The same thing happens in most of Lewis's big novels. In *Main Street,* Washington is attacked as much as Gopher Prairie; and in *Babbitt,* the reader is eventually brought around to a sympathetic appreciation of the middle-class businessman, while all the time the inadequacies of Babbitt's life-style are being pointed out.

This double-edged satire is suggestive, in its eastern-western aspects, of a conflict in Lewis himself, perhaps the major conflict in his life. He went east to school out of a belief that the culture, the polish, the ideas nec-

essary to success would be found there; and he did find
a tempo, a style that pleased him. It was his eastern experience that made him a man of the world and that influenced him socially throughout the rest of his life.
Frederick Manfred remarks on this influence in his recollection of an interview he had with Lewis in the
1940s: "He invited us in and was very cordial and warm
and a little mannered. I mean that in the sense of being
mannered different from the way we're mannered in the
Twin Cities. It was a manner that he probably picked up
in New York or Europe or somewhere, but you could
tell he'd been sanded over a little bit somewhere."[5]

It was not until Lewis returned to Minnesota and
the northern midwest for his settings and subject matter,
however, that he was able to make that crucial combination of style and content that meant success, a union involving the imposition of his eastern detachment and objectivity upon his native surroundings. But while this
synthesis worked in Lewis's writing, it did not work in
his personality. Thereafter, Lewis never seemed able to
decide whether he himself would act as if he were a so-
phisticate from New York or a rough-and-ready country
boy from Sauk Centre. So he became neither one nor the
other, always self-conscious and uncomfortable in the
big city and quickly bored when he went back home.
Lewis lived as if he were attending a finishing school
from which his own small-town background kept him
from graduating. One could even read Lewis's novels as
a search for a believable hero who can satisfactorily
combine the values of the frontier with the intellect of
the east—a hero that seems to be realized most fully in
Cass Timberlane (in the novel of that name).

But as much trouble as Lewis's eastern and western
impulses gave him, it was the return to his native
grounds, his commitment, as he indicated in an early

letter to Joseph Hergesheimer, to the "flat hungriness of
the Middle West,"[6] that brought together all of those
strange qualities that make a writer's work suddenly
seem, to use Norman Mailer's expression, "at dead center" and lead one to say, "Yes, this is about the way it
is."[7] And if one is inclined to think of Minnesota in
terms of literature at all, Sinclair Lewis is the name that
comes immediately to mind. Other Minnesotans have
been important writers, and among these F. Scott Fitzgerald has a critical reputation greater than that of
Lewis. But no other Minnesota writer has used Minnesota as a setting more significantly and notoriously than
did Sinclair Lewis.

Main Street, Cass Timberlane, Kingsblood Royal,
and *The God-Seeker* are set in Minnesota, and *The Trail
of the Hawk, Free Air, Babbitt,* and *Arrowsmith,* as well
as many of Lewis's short stories, have Minnesota scenes
or describe landscapes reminiscent of Minnesota. Lewis's use of Minnesota in his fiction was more than a
matter of the mingled attraction and dissatisfaction that
he felt toward his home state, which had such a lasting
influence on his life. With his eye for the unusual, an
ability developed during his years as a book editor, he
saw a unique quality in Minnesota. Lewis explained this
quality in the essay "Minnesota, the Norse State," which
appeared in *The Nation* for 30 May 1923 (an essay
that also underscores the east-west problem in Lewis's
thinking):

Minnesota is unknown to the Average Easterner, say to a
Hartford insurance man or to a New York garment-worker,
not so much because it is new as because it is neither Western and violent, nor Eastern and crystallized. Factories and
shore hotels are inevitably associated with New Jersey, cow-
punchers and buttes with Montana; California is apparent,
and Florida and Maine. But Minnesota is unplaced. I have

heard a Yale junior speculate: "Now you take those Minnesota cities—say take Milwaukee for instance. Why, it must have a couple of hundred thousand population, hasn't it?" (Nor is this fiction. He really said it.) [8]

It was the unplaced quality of Minnesota that fascinated Lewis, and it was this quality of the state that he exploited in his writing. Lewis wrote about Minnesota for an eastern audience as if it were a foreign country (Frank Norris did the same in writing about California). And in reading *Main Street* one has the feeling that he is taking a train ride into unexplored territory. Because so few of his readers knew what Minnesota was like or even where it was, Lewis was able to imprint his conception of the state in their minds. As E. M. Forster wrote in 1929, "I persist in exclaiming, for what Mr. Lewis has done for myself and thousands of others is to lodge a piece of the continent in our imagination." [9]

Minnesota is to an understanding of Lewis's writing much the same as Mississippi is to that of William Faulkner's or Algeria to that of Albert Camus's. It is at once a symbol and a state of mind, a stage on which Lewis saw being acted out those dramas most crucial to his conception of our eternal warfare with stupidity. It is, as Lewis wrote, "the newest empire of the world; the Northern Middlewest; a land of dairy herds and exquisite lakes, of new automobiles and tar-paper shanties and silos like red towers, of clumsy speech and a hope that is boundless." [10] It is as if Lewis saw Minnesota as the last chance for American civilization, the place where the struggle between the freedom of the prairies and the restraint of the drawing room might yet be worked out. "What is its future?" he asks. "The ancient stale inequalities or something different in history, unlike the tedious maturity of other empires? What future and what hope?" [11] But if he wanted to draw the attention of Americans to the nation's heartland, he also wanted to change the attitudes of Minnesotans toward Minnesota. He disliked the smug assurance on the part of so many Minnesotans that civilization in their state was progressing in the best possible way, and his satire is aimed at that smugness by way of warning.

Unlike Faulkner, Lewis could never settle permanently in his home territory after he had left it for the east, although he made sporadic attempts at relocating in Minnesota. He lived for periods of time in Saint Cloud (visiting Claude), Mankato, Saint Paul, Minneapolis, in a cabin on Big Pelican Lake, in Excelsior on the shore of Lake Minnetonka, and in Duluth. It was in Duluth that he made his most serious attempt at putting down roots, buying a large house overlooking Lake Superior (he sold the house the next year). He never maintained a residence for long in Minnesota as an adult, but he was a devoted student of Minnesota politics, lore, and geography. One of his favorite games, when encountering a fellow Minnesotan in a distant place, was to challenge him to name in order all the counties in the state, starting with the northern corner (Minnesota counties appear on the map stacked vertically in rows).

All sections of Minnesota and dozens of characters modeled on his observations of Minnesotans found their way into Lewis's writing. Actual places, disguised only in name, were captured in his photographic style. Sauk Centre, Mankato, Duluth, Minneapolis, Saint Paul, the farm country around Fergus Falls and Moorhead, and the northwoods of the Arrowhead (Minnesota's northeastern tip)—all appear in Lewis's works, as do their inhabitants. Lewis was permanently conscious of his home state, and he realized that his personality could be understood only in reference to the place where he was born. "I find myself thinking of its streets and its people and the familiar, friendly faces when I am on the great avenues of New York, or Paris, or Berlin, or Stockholm," he wrote in 1931. "To me, forever, *ten miles* will not be a distance in the mathematical tables, but slightly more than the distance from Sauk Centre to Melrose."[12]

Minnesota as the setting for Lewis's novels and the fabric of his vision is something that becomes more apparent the deeper one reads into Lewis's own comments on his compulsive return to his native grounds. "To understand America," he wrote in the early 1920s, "it is merely necessary to understand Minnesota."[13] This is no easy job, because as Lewis wryly added, "to understand Minnesota you must be an historian, an ethnologist, a poet, a cynic, and a graduate prophet all in one."[14]

Lewis's success in making Minnesota the crossroads of American culture in the 1920s is indicated by the agreement among many critics that if there was one thing Lewis was able to do, it was to understand America. As H. L. Mencken said in his review of *Babbitt,* Lewis chronicled the "real America."[15] Lewis's America seemed real to Mencken and other readers because Lewis was a student of the popular culture other writers with their more specific interest in Freudian psychology (Sherwood Anderson), mechanistic skepticism (Theodore Dreiser), and the nature of language (Gertrude Stein) ignored. As Vernon L. Parrington testified:

Mr. Lewis has been at enormous pains to gather his materials at their sources. He has taken upon himself to become a specialist in depicting the genus Americanus. He has loafed along Main Street, played poker in back rooms with wicked young men, drunk in respectable clubs, and exchanged hearty back-slappings with the sons of Rotary. He has devoted days to the smoking compartments of Pullmans, garnering the ripest wisdom and choicest stories of traveling salesmen. He has listened to philosophic brokers discourse on ethics, studied political and constitutional theory with realtors, learned all about Bolshevism from presidents of Chambers of Commerce, been instructed in the elements of economics by Republican congressmen, discovered the fallacies of Darwinian evolution from clerical fundamentalists and the superiority of Fascism over democracy from the greatest captains of industry. No field of American experience has escaped his minute investigation.[16]

Because of his willingness to find the materials for his fiction in the sources of popular culture, Lewis has been labeled a cartoonist, a reporter, and an amateur sociologist—all of which, to some extent, he was. But at the same time Lewis was one of the first writers to document and to understand the American fascination with the garish self-image reflected by the automobile-and-gadget dominated world that twentieth-century industrialism had produced by the 1920s, a fascination that developed into an art movement in the late 1950s. The minute and loving description Lewis gave to the FREE AIR signs that hung outside service stations in 1919, or the care with which he described Babbitt's silver-plated cigar lighter, was much the same as the impulse behind Jasper John's Ballantine Ale cans, Andy Warhol's Campbell's Soup painting, and the whole Pop Art scene.

Lewis's success as a chronicler of life in the 1920s did not come easily, despite the flippant quality of so much of his work and despite the way his books look at first as if they would be easy to write (just go back to your home town and watch what goes on and you will have a *Main Street,* just follow a businessman around for a day and you will have a *Babbitt*). Lewis's critics and imitators found, as did those of Warhol, that the soup can is simple to depict until one tries to do it. And

Lewis labored hard over his novels, as the word changes, notes, and erasures on his manuscripts show. Lewis gave an account of his labors in a 1921 essay entitled "How I Wrote a Novel on Trains and beside the Kitchen Sink." In that essay Lewis detailed how he was able to combine his early novel-writing with a full-time job in a publishing house. He got up early in the morning and wrote for an hour or so on the drainboard in the kitchen. He utilized the thirty-five to fifty minutes of commuting time to do some more writing on the train. When he lunched alone, he used his solitude to think up plots. On the way back home he would try to get a few more hundred words down, and then in the evening he would try to get in another hour or two. "I decided," he wrote, "that I would not have time for being tired, instead of not having time for writing."[17] Lewis had, in quantity at least, one thing that most writers lack—the willpower to write, no excuses permitted; that he produced twenty-three novels and two collections of short stories is not surprising.

Success, when it came to Sinclair Lewis, was thus about as deserved as it could be. Some 200,000 copies of *Main Street* were sold within a few months after its publication on 23 October 1920. The first printing of *Babbitt* (80,500 copies), which appeared on 19 September 1922, quickly sold out, and total sales rapidly climbed into six figures. Prepublication orders for *Arrowsmith* in March 1925 went over 50,000, and sales shot upward after publication. *Elmer Gantry,* issued on 10 March 1927, had the largest first printing (140,000 copies) of any book up to that time, and 175,000 copies were moved in little over a month. Although the sales of *Dodsworth,* which came out in March 1929, were damaged by the stock-market crash, the total reached 80,000 within four months. And Lewis's sales did not decline drastically even in the 1930s and 1940s: *Ann Vickers* (1933) sold over 130,000 copies; *It Can't Happen Here* (1935) sold 300,000; *Cass Timberlane* (1945) was a Book-of-the-Month-Club selection and sold over a million copies; and *Kingsblood Royal* (1947) sold over a million and a half copies.

The big money, the success that Lewis earned so suddenly at the very start of the 1920s, gave him trouble. The buoyancy that characterizes his letters up to 1920 is toned down after *Main Street,* partly because his achievements did not earn him the respect he had hoped for from other writers. In a letter to Joseph Hergesheimer he expressed discontent with what *Main Street* had brought him: "Every once in a while some friend indignantly tells me that some bunch of the young jeunes—say those at the Café Rotonde on the rive gauche—assert that if the damned book has sold so well, I must be rotten."[18] Lewis found himself in the position of the best-selling writer scorned by the literati because of the suspicion that any book that is popular must be artistically defective.

Even after he received the Nobel Prize for Literature in 1930, Lewis was bothered by the thought that it was his criticism of American society, not his skill as a writer, that influenced the Swedish Academy. And his failure to create a school of followers led to further self-doubt. It has often been suggested that he "influenced public thinking rather than public writing."[19] On this score one should remember, however, that Lewis's methods and satirical approach were not without at least some impact on the next generation of writers. John Steinbeck owed something to Lewis's research methods, especially in *The Grapes of Wrath,* and Nathanael West could not have written *A Cool Million* without some consciousness of *Babbitt*. But however one looks at it,

Lewis's success was anything but easy for him to handle.

It was after the triumphant appearance of *Main Street* that Lewis's difficulties with alcohol began. And his case at first seems to be a classic one—big money followed by heavy drinking and the dissolution of his marriage to Grace Hegger in 1928. (He married again in the same year, this time to political commentator Dorothy Thompson, a marriage that also ended in divorce, in 1942.) The accounts of Lewis's drinking bouts are many. He would invite guests to a dinner party and collapse before it was over (and sometimes before it started). He went on several binges with Thomas Wolfe in London—adventures that Wolfe later made use of in *You Can't Go Home Again*. All of this drinking was a source of despair to his friends. "Red had no particular time for drinking," wrote Sheean. "If he wanted a drink he would take it at any hour—starting, that is, when he got up in the morning."[20]

Such a regimen was devastating to Lewis's health. When he settled down to another book, the drinking would stop, and for long periods he restricted himself to iced coffee or, at worst, beer. Drink did not seem to be an uncontrollable habit for Lewis and there is some doubt, at least in the strict medical sense of the term, that he was an alcoholic. Why then did he drink so excessively? A plausible explanation is that he lived his most successful years during the era when drinking became a symbol of defiance for those writers who were part of Mencken's circle (it was, as Carl Bode pointed out, Prohibition that provoked some of Mencken's best writing and added greatly to his popularity[21]). Lewis's guzzling, like Mencken's, constituted a sneer at the same forces of blind puritanism that Lewis attacked in *Main Street* and *Babbitt*. And Lewis's first wife, Grace Hegger, talked about Lewis's drinking in the context of the boozing pattern that Prohibition imposed: "How much this sense of compulsion, this acting as if every drink were the last one, this adolescent excitement over breaking the law, how much this had to do with creating the drink habit for Lewis, it is impossible to know. But this national state of mind plus his own emotional dissatisfaction must have encouraged a craving which brought him again and again to death's door."[22]

Another and a deeper explanation for Lewis's drinking is that he escaped into alcohol to overcome his feelings of sexual inadequacy, what the first Mrs. Lewis called his emotional dissatisfaction. "In his heart of hearts," according to Sheean, "he had an awful involuntary humility which came from the conviction that he was unfit for, and perhaps even unworthy of, love in its fullness. His sexual nature suffered, to the very brink of impotence, through this physical humility. Alcohol as a refuge stilled the pain but only increased the condition which was its source."[23]

It is a mistake, however, to assume that Lewis's drinking was instrumental in leading to the failure of his marriages or in bringing about the problems he had with his writing after 1930. He was a writer who drank, not, as so many have believed, a drunk who wrote. His marital difficulties were undoubtedly compounded by the feelings of physical inferiority that stimulated his drinking; but the marriages seemed to fail ultimately for other reasons—incompatability of personality and Lewis's chronic inability to settle down to the commitments of a permanent home. The difficulty he had in maintaining his reputation as a writer during the last two decades of his life was more a consequence of changing times than a result of booze. Who among the writers of the 1920s survived the Depression any better than Lewis did? Popular decline was much more a reality for Mencken and

Fitzgerald than it was for Lewis. Compulsive drinking was never at the root of Lewis's problems. As Dorothy Thompson said, Lewis drank because he wanted to, not because he couldn't help it.[24]

Drinking, for Lewis, was a symptom, not a cause; and perhaps it was not even the major symptom. What Lewis seemed most unable to control was his impulsiveness. He liked to undertake a journey at a moment's notice, change residences overnight, abandon trips before they were half over, switch the topic of conversation abruptly, and even make a decision about his next novel, as he did with *Arrowsmith,* in the midst of an all-night drinking excursion. Lewis repeatedly felt compelled to say, "Let's go. . . . This place has no reality for me."[25] His restlessness was disturbing to both his wives. When Grace tried to talk him into buying a house of their own after their son was born, he objected, saying: "I don't want a home. I want to travel, to see, to feel."[26]

Lewis traveled and he saw, but there was a quality in his restlessness that made feeling difficult for him; like so many others whose lives can be read in hotel registers, he was driven by curiosity and fear. He set off on trips to Rome, California, the Canadian wilderness, and dozens of other places because he was incessantly curious about those places. And many of his novels can be read as travel books, tourists' guides to the small town, the midwestern city, the big woods, London, Paris, and Venice. Throughout Lewis's life he retained the boyish inquisitiveness that sent him on his cattle-boat trips during his Yale years; at the same time, he had anxieties over what he might find in himself if he stayed in one place too long. As soon as he had seen what there was to see in Verona, he would find himself looking inward, and he seemed to be both repelled and bored by what he saw, apparently more interested in the motives of others

than in his own. He felt considerable disgust with his
own image, a reaction that he experienced repeatedly
but never more symbolically than when he took dancing
lessons as a young man at Duryea's Academy in New
York, lessons "given by a bored young woman in a mir-
ror-lined room where he was horrified by his awkward-
ness from a hundred angles."[27] It was not that Lewis
wanted to escape from himself in all his traveling; it was
that he was one of those strange individuals who is not
much interested in his own personality. His books are
not, as a consequence, ego trips; in this respect he was
the opposite of a writer such as Thomas Wolfe.

Lewis has been attacked for his lack of introspec-
tion, his reluctance to bring himself into his novels. But
such an attack is largely unjustified because it was his
readiness to be the observer of things and people outside
himself that enabled him to be the kind of novelist and
engaging conversationalist that he was—more concerned
with what others think, feel, and do than with himself.
His friends often remarked on his ability to mimic
clergymen, politicians, and other writers—a source of humor Lewis sometimes carried too far. One afternoon,
over a bottle of whiskey at the Lafayette Hotel in New
York City, he decided to telephone Dorothy Thompson
and impersonate a German professor supposedly interested in getting her opinions on certain difficult passages
in Lewis's novels. The impersonation was successful
until he could not keep it up any longer. A few days
later a professor actually called Dorothy from Berlin
and began his conversation with the same request Lewis
had used. "Come off it, you son of a bitch," she said. "I
know you. You can't fool me again."[28]

Lewis's talent for capturing the accents and man-
nerisms of others led him into a mildly successful career
as an actor in the late 1930s and early 1940s (he had

parts in summer productions of Eugene O'Neill's *Ah,
Wilderness!* and Thornton Wilder's *Our Town,* played
the main part in a Federal Theater Project adaptation of
his novel *It Can't Happen Here,* and toured with the
company of his own play *Angela Is Twenty-Two*).
Lewis the actor, the mimic, the observer is also Lewis
the writer who, it is thought, "would never be able to
project in art the forms of his suffering, one who would
never wish to allow—if he could—his writing to confront
his subjectivity. . . ."[29]

But Lewis's reluctance to confront himself has
been, like most of his deficiencies, exaggerated. During
the last decade of his life there is evidence that he came
to terms with himself in several ways. Friends, such as
Frederick Manfred, who had opportunity to talk with
Lewis at length during the 1940s present a picture of a
man far different from that of the younger, edgy, dissatisfied, restless Lewis. Lewis apparently came to understand many of his own feelings of inferiority and to
see through them. He told Manfred, for example, that
"There was a time in my life when I was sure that with
this to look at [his face] anybody who said they loved
me were liars—said it because they had to."[30] Dorothy
Thompson, on another point and sounding, rather
coldly, like the author of a textbook in psychology, had
written to Lewis in 1937: "I know what is eating you
and always, periodically, has eaten you. It is the fear
that your creative power is waning."[31] But Lewis had
even come to grips with this fear, a fear that has devastated countless writers. As he said to Manfred:

"That's the way it goes. For a little while you have it. The
old bite, the old sting. And you give it to 'em while you
have it. And everybody cheers and everybody says, 'He's
really on today, isn't he? He's really hot this time! Wow!'
But it isn't long before it's all gone. The vim, the vigor, the
celestial spark. All gone."[32]

A tone of acceptance is audible in Lewis's remarks to Manfred, an acceptance of Lewis by Lewis.

Even the notion that Lewis did not write about himself in his novels should not be taken without qualification. Aspects of his personality appear in all of his books. It is more than a matter of speculation, for instance, that Carol Kennicott in *Main Street* is often Lewis himself. "Yes," Lewis once said, "Carol is 'Red' Lewis: always groping for something she isn't capable of attaining, always dissatisfied, always restlessly straining to see what lies just over the horizon, intolerant of her surroundings, yet lacking any clearly defined vision of what she really wants to do or to be."[33] In various ways, all of Lewis's protagonists embody the restless quality found in Carol (a restlessness that seems to develop out of self-dissatisfaction, the sense of inadequacy suggested by Grace Hegger). Babbitt longs for all the things the world of the small-time businessman lacks—manly adventure, passionate love, authentic dignity. Arrowsmith wants to get into the "pure" research that is all but denied to the twentieth-century scientist. Elmer Gantry, unable to be moral himself, wants to lead the nation toward morality. Dodsworth's European journey in search of love and old-world tastes in the company of a wife who understands neither is, in all respects, Lewis's most sophisticated treatment of the restlessness in himself.

In novel after novel during the 1930s and 1940s Lewis returned to the discontented hero: Ann Vickers searching for a compromise between her life as a career woman and her sexual needs; Gideon Planish wanting to remain an obscure and plodding professor but forced into a life of charlatanism; Cass Timberlane trying to find happiness with a girl twenty years younger than himself; and Kingsblood Royal trying to find some way of reconciling the racial hatred in the United States and its mani-

festations in himself. Lewis's lifelong need to seek new
places, his readiness to undertake a journey at a moment's notice, his despair over his own appearance and
his own accomplishments—all of this is found in his
novels.

The opinion that Lewis became a novelist who
could not write about his own suffering, one who could
not confront his own subjectivity, is most certainly
wrong. Lewis's last novel, *World So Wide,* published in
1951 after his death, brings together much of Lewis's
understanding of his own life and is proof that he did
come into confrontation with his subjectivity. The novel
was written while Lewis was living out the last two years
of his life, suffering from a worsening of the precancer-
ous skin condition that had tormented him for a long
time. He labored under the awareness that his best work
was behind him, that he, the novelist who had struggled
to be topical (and with great success almost to the end,
witness the huge sales of *Kingsblood Royal* in 1947)
was no longer in touch with the mood of his times. Both
of his marriages had gone bad, and of his sons one was
dead and the other had grown up with little fatherly
contact. Lewis had almost no close friends left, and alcohol had become a problem again.

Amid this suffering, Lewis worked on *World So
Wide,* the story of Hayden Chart, an architect from
Newlife, Colorado, who travels to Europe after his nagging wife is killed in an automobile accident (there is
some suggestion that Chart is responsible for the accident). Chart had wished for his wife's death because he
thought of her, with her social pretensions, as a bore.
But the basic reason for his dislike of her is something
else: she understands him better than he understands
himself. She accuses him of being a sexual coward and
a phony; by the end of the novel, after we have seen him

intimidated by women in the same manner as Mr.
Wrenn, Will Kennicott, Dodsworth, and Cass Timberlane before him, we realize that she is right. What Chart
cannot stand about his wife is the way she confronts him
with himself. So she is conveniently eliminated, and
Chart sails the Atlantic seeking answers to questions
that have already been answered for him; like the archetypal American in Europe, Chart believes that to gain
self-knowledge he must be willing to "burn his own
house, destroy his own city, so that he might in fiery
freedom see all of this world so wide."[34]

Hayden Chart, like Sinclair Lewis himself, is af-
flicted with a fever of discontent that is almost without
remedy. In a statement that must have been in Lewis's
mind for years before he wrote it down, Chart admits
that everything up to the "burn-off" point had been "a
dream of life in which he had been busy and important
and well-bedded and well-fed and had glowingly possessed everything except friends and contentment and
any reason for living: a dream, a fable, a caricature of
grandeur."[35] But Chart's departure for Europe in the
hope of finding his own beginnings in the beginnings of
Western civilization has a note of despair about it from
the start. "He was a tired man," Lewis wrote with evident self-consciousness:

too tired, surely, to make a new life or do anything but
regret the old life that he had known as safe and profitable.
. . . Already he knew what every exile before Dante or
since has had to learn: That in the whole world only a few
neighborly streets are interested in letting you live, and if
you challenge strangers, "But I have the high purpose of
exploring and conquering and colonizing my soul," they
yawn, "Oh, yes? But why do it here?"[36]

Chart becomes an exile, tries to study Italian history, falls in love with a medieval scholar who does not

love him, and finds it impossible to be assimilated into old world culture. It is not until the reappearance of a hometown girl, Roxanna Eldritch, who has failed as a newspaperwoman in Europe, that Chart is saved from his life of self-torture. And in Roxanna's rescue of Chart, Lewis finally worked out an ending that was psychologically satisfying to himself, an ending in which those problems that plagued him all his life—reluctance to look deeply into his own personality, a sense of being a stranger and an outsider everywhere he went, and his failure to find a woman with whom he could be happy— are resolved.

When Hayden Chart realizes that he has always loved Roxanna and marries her, the irony that has been latent from the start of the story (and the irony that is latent in Lewis's life) is defused. How ironic that the hero should have set out in search of a new life when he was already living in Newlife. How ironic that a man named Chart would have to search throughout the world for the map to his own life. And how ironic that an architect whose ambition was to "build that prairie village which was to have been all housed in one skyscraper: the first solution in history of rural isolation and loneliness"[37] should have gone to Europe to study cathedrals. Roxanna makes Chart realize that what he has been searching for is what he left behind; in burning his house he had very nearly succeeded in burning himself. Roxanna is America, the west, the small town, and there is "a sweet wild smell about her, like sagebrush."[38] She is the direct, sympathetic woman Chart had overlooked in marrying his first wife (whose name, significantly, was Caprice). Roxanna is everything Chart had rejected when he began his world wandering; yet she is everything he needs to understand himself, to cease being an outsider, and to become sexually balanced.

For Lewis himself, there was to be no Roxanna Eldritch and no new life. Like Chart, Lewis had arrived in Italy, but he was not to make a circumnavigation that would take him back to the American midlands. In *World So Wide* Lewis did achieve some consolation, however. He rewrote his own life, gave it the ending he wished for, and sensed where he had gone wrong. Such awareness came late and it came in a weak novel; but it is an awareness that does not come at all to many writers.

The patterns of Lewis's sufferings are there for us to see in his novels, but that is not why his novels were written (with the exception of *World So Wide*) nor is it why they are read. Lewis saw deeply enough into himself, for his life was not the blindly tragic life it has often been made out to be; but more importantly he saw deeply into the consciousness of his time and the makeup of his country.

Sinclair Lewis's life was not a particularly American one in that he did not burn himself out early, he never dropped out of public view (his death was front-page news in almost every American and European newspaper), and he was not the victim of a puritan conscience. But the development of his style and his search for a significant theme were distinctly American in his movement back toward the idiom and landscape of his native Minnesota, and it is this, not his life, that makes Lewis a writer of lasting importance in understanding America. One by one he turned to the topics that any student of American culture must first understand before he can understand anything—the small town, the businessman, the scientist, the preacher, the capitalist in search of culture, the latent fascism in American democracy, and race relations. And in turning to these topics, he helped his readers to become part of the intellectual movement that now seems to be the most significant part of twentieth-century American history, the development of a national self-awareness, but not, as we have seen, at the complete expense of his own personality. Lewis was lonely and Lewis was hunted by his critics; but he was not destroyed by his loneliness or by his critics.

2

"Moralities for a New Time"

We are unsettled to the very roots of our being. There isn't a human relation, whether of parent and child, husband and wife, worker and employer that doesn't move in a strange situation.

—Walter Lippmann, *Drift and Mastery: An Attempt to Diagnose the Current Unrest*

A disquieting strangeness was apparent to Americans in 1920. The educated young housewife feeling trapped in a small town on the plains; the real-estate broker driving to work on a spring morning; the health officer making his rounds in an Iowa town; the Methodist preacher thinking up a new fund-raising scheme; and the automotive engineer with marital problems—all were conscious of being in strange situations. William E. Leuchtenburg, the historian of the 1920s, has written that for the first time, Americans were "confronted with the need to fashion instruments and attitudes appropriate to an economy of abundance."[1] The old economy of scarcity that had made puritan attitudes toward work and pleasure appropriate and perhaps even necessary was destroyed by the boom economy brought on by World War I. The Jeffersonian notion of a nation centered on the farm and the small-town had been forsaken in favor of the urbanized industrial state. Isolation, which had been so much a part of American consciousness, was being attacked in all its forms—rural isolation by the automobile, the radio, and the telephone; and national isolation by the rise of the United States to world power (despite the widespread desire to return to pre-war insularity). A new time had come demanding a new consciousness and a new way of living—and to many Americans, the demands seemed to be too great, as did the confusion over how to live in a world suddenly full of gadgetry, liberated women, and politicians who stood for normalcy instead of heroism. An interpreter of change was needed, someone who could explain what had happened and suggest ways of dealing with the sudden strangeness. Sherwood Anderson and H. L. Mencken partially fulfilled this need; but it was Sinclair Lewis who seemed to offer the most.

Lewis has been understood as a satirist, a muckraker, a humorist, a realist, a naturalist, and a cartoonist. But the best way to explain his popularity and influence during the 1920s is to see him as a moralist. Alfred Kazin has interpreted Lewis's work in the 1930s as "moralities for a new time,"[2] but it is even more important and necessary to interpret the novels of Lewis's big decade in the same way. In *Main Street, Babbitt, Arrowsmith, Mantrap, Elmer Gantry, The Man Who Knew Coolidge,* and *Dodsworth* Lewis was ultimately concerned with the question of how to live in American culture of the 1920s rather than with what that culture was like. The objective in his writing, however satirically he may have intended it, is indicated in the title of the last chapter of *The Man Who Knew Coolidge,* published in 1928: "The Basic and Fundamental Ideals of Christian American Citizenship." Like his own Lowell Schmaltz, the garrulous businessman who delivers a 275-page monologue in the novel, Lewis tried "to outline in a simple way the ethics of the New Generation—of the New American Era."[3]

He began with *Main Street,* which came out in October of 1920. The plot of *Main Street* is so unembellished that the setting, Gopher Prairie, a central Minnesota town of some two thousand inhabitants, becomes as important as what happens to the characters in the story. Carol Kennicott, the heroine, is a Saint Paul librarian who marries Gopher Prairie physician Will Kennicott. Lewis then proceeded to give a cross section of life in a midwestern small town as seen through Carol's eyes. In a series of encounters she becomes acquainted with almost everyone in Gopher Prairie: the Dave Dyers and the Sam Clarks of the business class; the Champ Perrys of the old pioneering class; Guy Pollock, the aging radical lawyer; Miles Bjornstam, the village atheist; Vida Sherwin, the schoolteacher, and many others. Carol is soon caught in a love-hate relationship with the town and its people. She is depressed to the point of a near breakdown by the dullness of provincial life; at the same time she is stirred by the beauty of the countryside and the solidity of her plain-spoken but sometimes heroic physician husband—a solidity she, for all her liberal sentiments, lacks. At last, distressed by her failure to reform Gopher Prairie through various schemes to intellectualize the ladies' literary society (the Thanatopsis Club), renovate the village architecture, increase the public library holdings, and sustain a little-theater group, she leaves with her small son, Hugh, for Washington, D.C. and work in the war effort. She finds, however, that the big city is nearly as dull as Gopher Prairie. She becomes homesick, and Dr. Kennicott wins her back. Carol returns home, but she makes it clear that her capitulation is not complete. She is still uncertain about the possibilities for happiness in middle America.

Contrary to what many critics have assumed, *Main Street* was not addressed to the spirit of youthful revolt that followed the Armistice of 1918. When the story of Carol Kennicott ends, she is middle-aged, middle-aged in 1920; and it is to Carol's generation, the generation in power, that *Main Street* and all of Lewis's 1920s novels are addressed. This at once sets Lewis off from the younger writers of the era such as Fitzgerald and Hemingway, and also explains much of their discontent with him. Lewis's heroes are people who grew up with progressivism, fed upon the liberalism of Upton Sinclair and the economics of Thorstein Veblen, and sat through World War I on the home front. "Life had begun with war" for Fitzgerald and Hemingway, "and would forever after be shadowed by violence and death."[4] But life had begun for Lewis with the prewar optimism of the socialist vision, and he never lost his belief that the United States could become civilized through an awakening of the social conscience of the middle class. Socialism in America has historically differed from communism in directing its revolutionary efforts at the middle class instead of advocating destruction of that class in favor of the proletariat. This is why Lewis's novels are aimed at Matthew Arnold's philistines—the doctors' wives, the businessmen, the scientists, the preachers—in an attempt to explain to them, as Lewis wrote late in 1914, why "almost all of the people who do think are agreed that things are not as they should be; that education is either absurd or weightily inefficient; that under the present economic system—technically called 'capitalism'—products do not get distributed as they should."[5]

Perhaps there was not enough national wealth prior to 1920 to provide the comforts of the modern society for everybody: some people had to be content to do without. When Carol proposes to Mrs. Champ Perry at a meeting of the Thanatopsis Club that they modernize the tawdry rest room Gopher Prairie provided for the farmers' wives, Mrs. Perry says: "When Champ and I came here we teamed-it with an ox-cart from Sauk Centre to Gopher Prairie, and there was nothing here then but a stockade and a few soldiers and some log cabins. When we wanted salt pork and gunpowder, we sent out a man on horseback, and probably he was shot dead by the Injuns before he got back."[6] She goes on to say that nobody—and she was a farm wife herself in those days—expected any rest room at all.

Again and again when Carol proposes reform in

Gopher Prairie, whether the proposal is for more library
books or a remodeling project for the buildings along
Main Street, the answer she gets is much the same—compared to pioneer times, things are pretty good the way
they are now; besides, improvement would be too expensive. Carol tries unsuccessfully to convince the ruling
powers in Gopher Prairie that the economy has changed,
that there is enough money to go around, that the old
pioneer mentality and its obsession with scarcity is no
longer essential, that it is no longer necessary to live like
the old settlers who got through the winters by eating
rutabagas "raw and boiled and baked and raw again."[7]
She suggests to her husband that the farmers ought to
have a fairer share of the material benefits enjoyed by
the townspeople, but such a notion is all but incompre-
hensible to him. "Where'd the farmers be without the
town?" he asks. "Who lends them money? Who—why,
we supply them with everything!"[8] "Everything," of
course, amounts to little more than the bare necessities
of life on the frontier.

Lewis knew the strangeness the world of 1920 held
for middle-aged people, people who had been born,
after all, when the northern midwest was still largely
wild and unsettled. Frederick Jackson Turner had made
his pronouncements about the death of the frontier in
the 1890s, but the frontier consciousness with its sense
of struggle and its principle of reward (a man deserves
only what he has worked hard to obtain) remained alive.
John Smith's pronouncement at Jamestown that "if you
don't work you don't eat" became obsolete with the ar-
rival of an economy of abundance, but few members of
the middle class were ready to make the necessary ad-
justments in the year that *Main Street* was published.
Like so many of the economic assumptions Lewis chal-
lenged, the economy of scarcity was attacked because

with changing times it had become worse than outdated; it had become immoral.

The real shock value of *Main Street* thus lay not in its naturalistic exposé of life in a small town, but in its attempt to suggest how outmoded, how immoral, were some of the moral principles upon which the town and the nation itself had been founded and survived.

It was up to Carol's generation more than it had been to any other in American history to confront the inadequacy of the values and the solutions that were given to them as they grew up. *Main Street,* it must be remembered, is the history of a generation. The novel begins in 1906 when the "days of pioneering, of lassies in sunbonnets, and bears killed with axes in piney clearings, are deader now than camelot" and the American middlewest is a "bewildered empire."[9] This bewilderment is reiterated throughout the novel, first in Carol who cannot make up her mind about what sort of work she should do, and later in Kennicott and other citizens of Gopher Prairie who are driven to reject, out of frustration, the one principle that came automatically to their lips whenever they thought of the glories of their homeland: freedom. As Kennicott says to Carol in the argument that leads to their separation, "There's too much free speech and free gas and free beer and free love and all the rest of your damned mouthy freedom, and if I had my way I'd make you folks live up to the established rules of decency even if I had to take you—"[10]

Kennicott is echoing, in his own way, the same thing Walter Weyl expressed in his 1912 book, *The New Democracy*: "America is in a period of clamor, of bewilderment, of an almost tremulous unrest. We are hastily reviewing all our social conceptions. We are profoundly disenchanted."[11] On one side was great eco-

nomic growth, the gross national product rising from
$30.4 billion in 1910 to $71.6 billion in 1920. But on
the other side was the clamor of labor unrest (there were
over 2,000 strikes during the first half of 1916), demonstrations for women's rights, racial equality, leftist agitation, and World War I itself, the irony of which soon became apparent when the democratic principles the
United States was fighting for—freedom of the press, free
speech, and free thought—were curtailed at home in the
name of patriotism.

A last-ditch effort was being made to buttress the
old values inherent in the pioneer mentality, and the results were Prohibition, the witch-hunting conservatism
that brought about the Big Red Scare (the night of 2
January 1920, when Attorney General A. Mitchell
Palmer arrested some 5,000 alleged communists in simultaneous raids in cities across the country), a revived
Ku Klux Klan and other fascist organizations, and the religious fundamentalism manifested in the 1925 Scopes
Monkey Trial. But the inadequacy of the values that
came out of the rural state of mind was soon apparent,
as *Main Street* so timely testified. Sinclair Lewis knew
what Carol's generation had been through because he
was a member of it himself, and it was this quality of
sympathy that made him so appealing to an audience
made up largely of the same kind of people who appear
in the novel—the Carols and Wills, the Dyers, the Sam
Clarks, and even the Guy Pollocks—the solid, respectable, middle-class people who were running things.

By 1920, however, most of those people were not
living in the Gopher Prairies; they were in the cities, and
Lewis chose such a setting for *Babbitt,* which came out
in September 1922. As in *Main Street,* the locale of
Babbitt is almost as important as the story itself. Zenith
is a medium-sized American city in the imaginary mid-

western state of Winnemac, which figures again and again in Lewis's novels. We are given a detailed picture of life in Zenith through the characterization of George F. Babbitt, a fortyish real-estate executive and representative middle-class American. Babbitt has a pleasant house, a good car, a devoted if boring wife, two daughters and a son, a thriving business (in the management of which Babbitt is not always honest), a large circle of friends and acquaintances (including one very close friend, Paul Riesling, a frustrated violinist who earns his living as a roofing salesman), and a growing income.

Babbitt, despite recurring and disturbing erotic dreams involving a female "fairy child," is complacent until his existence is shaken by a sudden turn in Paul Riesling's discontentment. Riesling moves from philandering to violence, shoots his wife, Zilla, in the shoulder, and winds up in prison. Babbitt, mulling over Paul's actions, becomes aware of his own dissatisfactions; he starts to doubt that he is living in the best of worlds. His business associates begin to suspect him of being a renegade—and he gives them cause. He tries to regain pioneer vitality through a pilgrimage into the Maine wilderness. He has an affair with the lively widow Tanis Judique and nearly destroys his marriage. But he also develops sympathy for the plight of the working classes in Zenith. At the end, however, he is pressured economically, socially, and emotionally, into conforming once again. Yet he is able to assert himself in painful freedom and honesty when, on the last page, he backs the decision of his son Ted to do what he really wants and not be forced into going to college and taking the accepted bourgeois route to success and boredom.

Like Babbitt, a large percentage of urban Americans in the 1920s had come from small towns on the order of Gopher Prairie or Catawba (Babbitt's own hometown), and they carried much of the pioneer mentality with them. Babbitt repeatedly pays homage to the ideals of frugality and hard work, although he has no need to practice either and is revolted whenever he confronts his countrified half-brother Martin, who is a living representative of the old economy, "proud of being a freeborn independent American of the good old Yankee stock; he was proud of being honest, blunt, ugly, and disagreeable."[12] Such ideals are more out of place in Zenith than in Gopher Prairie, but they have their uses when employed by the businessmen against the workers. Babbitt's capitalist friends, and even Babbitt himself at first, attribute their comfortable lives to their own hard work and not to the exploitation of underpaid employees. When the telephone operators and linemen are joined in their strike by the dairy-products workers and the truck drivers, with talk of a trolley strike and a printers' strike, most members of Babbitt's circle look upon the union demands as little more than an attempt to take bread and butter off the middle-class table. They do not seem to realize that there is sufficient food for everyone; their mentality differs little from that of Will Kennicott. In Gopher Prairie revolution was not much of a threat, but union agitation nearly succeeds in shutting Zenith down. Lewis emphasized that the failure to comprehend the need for economic revision could not continue if the American city was to become a viable institution.

But instead of adjusting to the new realities of the industrial state, the executives of Zenith join forces to form the Good Citizens League, a nationwide organization designed to keep "the decent people in the saddle."[13] The objective of the Good Citizens League is to enforce conformity to business ideals, to pressure members of the establishment who might have some liberal tendencies to abide by the traditional way of doing business. The status quo, standardization, and repression of free speech are what the Good Citizens League stands for. It is, in a sense, the Commercial Club of Gopher Prairie expanded into a coast-to-coast operation, the small-town mind's way of comprehending and dealing with urbanization and surplus value.

In giving the Good Citizens League such an important role in *Babbitt* Lewis was drawing attention to the fascist tendencies that are constantly on the verge of destroying freedom in the United States. These tendencies can also be seen in Lewis's League of Cultural Agencies in *Arrowsmith,* as well as in the National Association for the Purification of the Arts and the Press (Napap) of *Elmer Gantry,* and reach their logical extension in the "Corpo" regime of *It Can't Happen Here.* The movement toward fascism in Babbitt's Zenith makes the book in effect a prologue to George Orwell's *1984,* and like *1984, Babbitt* is a document of alarm. Babbitt's speech before the Real Estate Board thus exists as a kind of warning: "I tell you," orates Babbitt, "Zenith and her sister-cities are producing a new type of civilization."[14] But the new type of civilization he has in mind is a standardized one with all of the cities, stores, hotels, clothing, and people (within their own classes) just alike.

Babbitt does show some resistance to joining the Good Citizens League, however, and in his discontentment with the life of conspicuous consumption and Chamber-of-Commerce hoopla he leads, he makes some beginnings toward a saner way of living. He not only comes to a more compassionate view of the striking workers; he also comes to a better understanding of what his friend Paul calls the "sweet, clean, respectable, moral life."[15] Like Riesling, Babbitt learns that business

morality consists mostly of cutting each other's throats
and making the public pay for it, and that the patterns of
behavior the members of the Zenith Athletic Club practice lead to boredom and even suicide. "Why do you
suppose so many Substantial Citizens jumped right into
the war?" Riesling asks. "Think it was all patriotism?"[16]

Babbitt tries to make his escape from respectability
in various ways—retreating to the Maine woods, having
an affair with Tanis Judique, and nearly throwing in his
lot with Seneca Doane, the radical lawyer and socialist
agitator. The forces of coercion are great and Babbitt is
unable to break away, but Lewis clearly established the
need to fulfill the longing for a more vital life than twentieth-century business culture offers. Babbitt's America
is a nation cultivating the death wish, but Babbitt des-
perately wants to choose life, a choice that must begin
with the decision to be free. Babbitt admits at the end
that in his whole life he has never done a single thing he
has wanted to, that he has never been able to make the
crucial decision that would have made him a hero instead of a fool. He is able to support his son's decision
not to go to college only because he has learned that
moral life must have a new definition. The social conscience of Babbitt, the typical middle-class businessman,
has been awakened.

Babbitt's inability to choose is a deficiency that
Lewis's next hero, Martin Arrowsmith, does not share.
Arrowsmith is first seen as a small-town boy who idol-
izes the local doctor and subsequently enters the Winnemac University Medical School. There he finds another
doctor to idolize, this time Max Gottlieb, a monomani-
acal but thorough research scientist whose example
dominates the rest of Arrowsmith's life. Arrowsmith
marries Leora Tozer, a student nurse, goes through a
number of jobs (general practitioner in Wheatsylvania,

North Dakota; health officer in Nautilus, Iowa; and eventually research fellow in the prestigious McGurk Institute in New York City). He goes to the West Indian island of Saint Hubert to apply the results of his research against a plague epidemic. The plague proves fatal to Leora, and the crisis of her death almost destroys Arrowsmith; but his dedication to scientific inquiry drives him on. He returns to his work, takes Joyce Lanyon, a rich socialite, as a second wife, and is seemingly set for life. But he feels compromised by the bureaucratic structure of the institute and decides at last to resign his position, leave his wife, and go to work in a small, independent laboratory in the Vermont woods.

Arrowsmith's story can be seen as a succession of right decisions—the right wife, the right career, and finally, in his giving up a prestigious position to work in an independent laboratory, the right course for the truth seeker to follow. But Arrowsmith has to deal with the same society that oppressed Babbitt, a society seemingly organized to prevent individual action, free thought, and pure research. Again and again Arrowsmith has to struggle against practicality—it is impractical for him to get married as a medical student; it is impractical for him to leave his growing practice in North Dakota to become a public-health officer; it is impractical for him to become a research fellow; and it is impractical for him to defy the American scientific establishment, with its institutions and grants, to set up a private laboratory. He finds himself continually pressured into endorsing practical applications of his researches, even though he knows that it is dishonest science to release findings before the consequences are known. Arrowsmith retains his independence to the end despite great psychological stress and at great personal cost (the loss of his first wife, the breakup of his second marriage), and his story is much more one of strength than is Babbitt's. The threat to Arrowsmith's freedom is perhaps also more severe than is the threat to Babbitt's freedom. It is bad enough for the American businessman to be denied independent action; it may be worse for the American scientist, upon whose thinking so much of the future depends, to be denied his independence. Out of this denial comes much of the tension in the book; for Arrowsmith, whose constant instinct is toward the moral choice, is continually being pressured toward abnegation of the moral responsibility that his profession demands.

Arrowsmith is hounded partly by the pioneer notion that a physician should be a setter of broken bones and a prescriber of medicine instead of a scientist; but he is also oppressed by the discovery that there is money to be made out of what goes on in the laboratory. Both sources of torment come out of the same idea—that a man ought to produce something tangible or he is no good and his work is without value. He comes close to losing his practice when one of his patients dies during Arrowsmith's brief career as a country doctor. And the worth of his work on bacteria is questioned when it does not lead immediately to a cure for disease and profits for the drug manufacturers. Like Carol and like Babbitt, a good part of Arrowsmith's struggle is against economic concepts that are outdated and immoral.

Arrowsmith performed a great service for Americans in the way it introduced them to twentieth-century medicine and the kind of research behind it. Lewis was the first novelist to deal in anything like an accurate and detailed manner with what goes on behind the laboratory door, and as a consequence he made his readers aware of processes that were ultimately to change their lives. The work of the scientist has determined to a large extent the way we live now, and Lewis captured a sense of that influence during the decade when it was beginning to be felt. He also suggested an outlet for the pioneer impulse, which seemed to be a doomed and frustrated thing in *Main Street* and *Babbitt*.

Pioneering, going back to nature, and the American tendency to seek out fulfillment and regeneration through roughing it received a consideration of a different sort in *Mantrap,* published in 1926. *Mantrap* has as its hero a New York lawyer named Ralph Prescott, whose nerves have been jangled by life in the city. He lets himself be talked into taking a fishing and canoeing trip along the Manitoba-Saskatchewan border with E. Wesson Woodbury, a raucous caricature of the sportsman as boor. At Mantrap Landing, a hunting and fishing outpost run by Joe Easter, an experienced and authentic woodsman, Prescott meets and falls in love with Alverna, Easter's wife. The triangle develops, and Prescott and Alverna find themselves on their own in the wilderness when she pursues him on an abortive trip in search of Woodbury, who is presumed lost. Prescott discovers courage he never knew he had as they survive starvation and a forest fire (along with some last-minute help from Easter). At the end of the novel Prescott gives Alverna up, which leaves him a stronger and wiser man.

Mantrap is overwritten and full of silly sentences and sentiments. The novel is overwhelmingly put down in most evaluations of Lewis. Writing in reference to the Pulitzer Prize Lewis refused for *Arrowsmith,* Mark Schorer stated, "Nothing in *Mantrap* suggests that its author was worthy of any prize, even the booby prize of *Broom*."[17] D. J. Dooley wrote: "In this 'shorter and more adventurous book,' there was very little that was not shoddy."[18] And Sheldon Grebstein was no kinder: "The book's humor is labored, its situations contrived, its tone so facetious it sometimes borders on self-

parody."[19] Joseph Wood Krutch was one of the few contemporary critics who defended the novel. *Mantrap* has
become one of the least-known and least-read of all
Lewis's works.

   Mantrap does continue a theme, however, that runs
through the works of Lewis, a theme involving the relationship between life in the wilderness of the city and
life in the primordial wilderness of the North American
continent. Babbitt, Arrowsmith, and even Carol Kennicott have their moments of retreat to the woods or
prairies, moments in which they hope to be revitalized
by taking on some of the energy their ancestors had
when they conquered the wild places. Lewis understood
the appeal of the wilderness, and he was not being un-
sympathetic in having Paul Riesling say of the Maine
back country: "Oh, it's darn good. There's something
eternal about it."[20] And when Lewis was a boy in Sauk
Centre he had heard grownups talk about escape not in
terms of the west but of the north, the direction of the
big woods. But he could not help pointing out the folly
in the notion that the wilderness is a place where a man
can fill his lungs with fresh air and become imbued with
manliness. Lewis often talked about the north woods,
and like Babbitt he had a romantic attitude toward it—
in his talk. But when he got back into the woods himself,
as he did in 1924 when he accompanied his brother
Claude on a trip with a Canadian government treaty
party into the same area described in *Mantrap,* he was
depressed by the stillness, the isolation, the boredom,
and the mosquitoes. So in addition to debunking life in
the small town and making fun of the business culture of
the city, Lewis did not let the call of the wild escape the
thrust of his satire.

   What Lewis debunked in *Mantrap* is what Prescott
calls "the most blatant of all our American myths:

roughing it in the wilds!"[21] This is a myth that is given credence by the suspicion of many Americans that their forebears, who took their ease in the wilderness, were hardier than they. It is also supported out of reaction to the great mythmaker Thoreau. Lewis often claimed to admire Thoreau, and in the struggles most of Lewis's characters—especially Babbitt, Arrowsmith, and Prescott —have against the moral coercion of middle-class life, we can see Lewis following Thoreau in speaking out against conformity. But Lewis shows, as Thoreau does not, how difficult it is to break loose. Babbitt is a good example. For a man in Babbitt's position, economic and social survival depend on conforming to a way of life quite different from that of the backwoodsman. And if Babbitt should turn his back on all, where would he go? He is out of place in the woods, and he, like Ralph Prescott, learns that the wilderness offers little possibility for redemption, nor is it even a satisfying escape. The only solution is more civilization, not less. Walden Pond is not as plausible in the twentieth century as it was in the nineteenth. *Mantrap* seems to exist as a correction to the implausibly romantic ending of *Arrowsmith,* even though it is sacrilege for most Americans to agree with Prescott that "fishing is dull and poker is duller, and . . . sleeping on the ground is pure *rot!*"[22]

Sacrilege is a word that was used often in the violent arguments that accompanied the publication in 1927 of *Elmer Gantry.* Lewis's version of what passed for religion in the United States of the 1920s brought him threats against his life and gave his name the same rhetorical function in Protestant fundamentalist sermons as that of Clarence Darrow, Darwin, and the devil himself. *Elmer Gantry,* like *Arrowsmith,* is an account of career development. At the start of the novel Elmer is a college football player so little given to piety that he is known as "Hell-cat." At the end of the book he is Dr. Gantry, minister of the large Wellspring Methodist Church in Zenith, with hopes of becoming the head of a national moral-rearmament organization, the National Association for the Purification of the Arts and the Press (Napap). But unlike Arrowsmith, Elmer Gantry's rise is depicted negatively. His decision to enter the ministry is dishonest and contrary to his own nature, and it costs him the respect and friendship of his agnostic college roommate, Jim Lefferts. Every decision Elmer makes thereafter is one of compromise. Early in his preaching career he jilts a country girl who loves him and whom he has seduced. He has an affair with female evangelist Sharon Falconer, which ends with her death in a flaming tabernacle. He marries a woman he does not love. And he has involvements with several of his church secretaries. Yet through it all, he is awarded ecclesiastical advancement, even though he barely escapes ruin at the conclusion of the novel when one of his secretaries, Hettie Dowler, tries to blackmail him. But while Elmer's career ascends, that of the honest Frank Shallard, who goes to the seminary with Elmer, descends to the point where Frank is beaten up by members of the Ku Klux Klan for preaching what he believes to be the truth.

Elmer Gantry, like all of Lewis's big novels, is part of one program. In it he established ties with *Main Street, Babbitt,* and *Arrowsmith.* He dealt with the connection between small-town provinciality and the religious proclivities of the time, the relationship between the gospel of Christianity and the gospel of business; and, because the novel was written out of the atmosphere surrounding the Scopes Monkey Trial, he dealt with the conflict between science and religion. But what perhaps made *Elmer Gantry* seem like such an act of outrage to so many readers is that Lewis did not simply

treat religion in relation to other aspects of American
life; he saw it instead as the molder of basic attitudes,
most of which were, in his opinion, bad.

Lewis made the point that Protestantism has nurtured America in the same way it has nurtured Elmer. It
has provided much of his and America's taste in architecture, clothing, music, literature, philosophy; it has
provided everything but "any longing whatever for decency and kindness and reason."[23] In *Elmer Gantry*
Lewis suggested that what is wrong with the small town,
what is wrong with business practices, and even what is
wrong with the intellectual attitudes that make it difficult
for the scientist to go about his research honestly are all
due to the hold Protestantism has on American consciousness. The one completely positive character in the
book, Frank Shallard, wants to make Christianity an active force for social good; as it is, it is a negative force, a
threat to freedom. Like Matthew Arnold, whose thinking Lewis often paralleled, Lewis maintained that He-
braism has too much prevailed over Hellenism and that
what is needed is more sweetness and light (Elmer, with
his black hair and black eyes, is, of course, the enemy of
light). Lewis said, flatly enough, that religion in the
United States has become stifling; that, like the pioneer
economy and the pioneer mentality of which it is a
manifestation, it has become a threat instead of a benefit.

The impact of religion on Elmer Gantry symbolizes
what it has done to the American spirit. At the beginning of the novel, Elmer is drunk, but he is drunk only
in the fashion of a hell-raising college boy who talks a
little like Huck Finn (his companion, perhaps significantly, is named Jim). But soon the church tightens its
grip on him; and for Elmer, there is no possibility of
lighting out for the territory. He is coerced into becoming a minister because his family, his town, and his col-

lege are so tightly structured around the church. Elmer
is beset on all sides; his mother, the YMCA, the president of the college, even a visiting evangelist—all single
him out in their prayers and exhortations. He relents
and the dark fabric of the preacher's suit is draped over
a body that is full of blind, yet healthy and normal impulses. The result is as discouraging, as horrifying, as it
would have been if Huck had been converted by Miss
Watson's Bible stories.

Elmer Gantry, like the big Lewis novels that pre-
ceded it, is centrally concerned with the struggle between
the old and the new. In a sense it is more centrally concerned because the pull between the old American and
the new American was so apparent in the religious con-
troversies of the time. A modernist movement, led by
such preachers as Harry Emerson Fosdick and reinforced by the essays that appeared in *The Christian
Century,* was concerned with making the church more
of a live option for the intellectual and the sophisticated
city dweller. Opposition to the movement was vicious;
Fosdick was ousted from his New York pulpit, and in
the Bible Belt and the deep south, fundamentalism
cranked itself up into a powerful machine that found expression through anti-evolution measures volumes of blue
laws, and the Ku Klux Klan. As the years went on, however, compromises were reached, and these can be seen
in the career of Elmer, who begins as a fundamentalist
and winds up as the pastor of a large, urban church. He
retains his theological naïveté, however, and it is clear
that his modernism is not sufficient.

But Elmer does have a program in Napap, which
he hopes will make him something of a moral dictator.
The purpose of Napap is "to make life conform to the
ideals agreed upon by the principal Christian Protestant
denominations."[24] This would be accomplished by com-

bining into one association all the moral organizations in America—the Anti-Saloon League, the Lord's Day Alliance, the Watch and Ward Society, and the Methodist Board of Temperance, Prohibition, and Public Morals—and then lobbying for legislated morality. Napap would bring about nationwide censorship of novels, plays, paintings, and movies. It would end Sunday entertainment, curtail freedom of speech, and put restrictions on the rights of Catholics. The result would be the fascist state against which *Babbitt,* in anticipation of *1984,* warns. At the end of the novel, Elmer is on bended knee, praying, "We shall yet make these United States a moral nation!"[25] The irony in Elmer's last statement underscores the immorality of the kind of enforced morality Elmer has in mind. It also underscores what Lewis saw as one of the greatest dangers in American society—the tendency toward excess not only in religion but also in production, consumption, patriotism, and the proliferation of institutions.

There is an air of excess in Lewis's next novel, *The Man Who Knew Coolidge,* that makes it a logical sequel to *Elmer Gantry.* The sheer wordiness of Lowell Schmaltz, who carries on a series of monologues that run for two hundred seventy-five pages, is one aspect of this excess. But the final section of the book, a speech Schmaltz delivers before the Men's Club of the Pilgrim Congregational Church (with Dr. Elmer Gantry appropriately in attendance), is even more excessive in the treatment given to the topic of Americanism. Schmaltz outlines what he calls "The Basic and Fundamental Ideals of Christian American Citizenship," which are service and practicalness. Service, according to the unwitting Schmaltz, is what the businessman employs to make up for shoddy goods. "The grocery customer will often prefer a second-rate apple in a handsome wrapper

to a first-rate one carelessly bundled in plain tissue paper," Schmaltz says. "A motorist will stand for pretty bad gasoline if the gas-station employees wear handsome uniforms, greet the customer respectfully, and wipe off his windshield free."[26] Practicalness is explained this way: "Europe has always had its art, its beauty, but where we have gone beyond the Old Country is that while we want things beautiful—take like an elegant new gas stove—they must be primarily of *use*."[27] Schmaltz combines the boorishness of Will Kennicott, Babbitt, and Elmer Gantry into a grotesque defense of almost all the déclassé attitudes of the 1920s. His speech, along with his earlier reminiscences, offers a startling collage of the words and ideas of Billy Sunday, Warren Harding, A. Mitchell Palmer, Calvin Coolidge, Bruce Barton, and Hiram Wesley Evans (the Imperial Wizard of the Ku Klux Klan during much of the 1920s).

Schmaltz's references to Europe point toward Lewis's next novel, *Dodsworth,* published in 1929. Sam Dodsworth, an automotive engineer and expresident of a corporation who possesses some Babbitt-Schmaltz characteristics and is married to a discontented wife named Fran, goes to Europe to determine, among other things, the validity of the excessive pride he has had in things American. He goes through a series of disenchantments with Fran, his country, and himself before realizing that he must abandon his unfaithful wife to her fate and begin a new life with Edith Cortright, a kind and sensible widow who represents the best in both European and American culture.

The device of taking his hero to Europe gave Lewis the opportunity to bring together much that he had been saying about the United States in his earlier novels. It is, of course, a device that had been used many times before, most notably in Mark Twain's *Innocents Abroad,* William Dean Howells's *Indian Summer,* Edith Whar-

ton's *The Custom of the Country,* and in several novels by Henry James including *The Ambassadors* and *The American.* But those are all older books, dealing with a European-American relationship that had changed greatly by 1925, the year in which *Dodsworth* is set. The Europe Lewis wrote about was a Europe greatly shaken by World War I and in debt both financially and psychologically to the United States. An American like Sam Dodsworth, given his success as an engineer and a business executive, can cross the Atlantic with doubts about the superiority of European culture and not feel that they result from mere provincialism. At the same time, Dodsworth is uncertain about the kind of life he has led in the United States. When he was a young man (the novel opens in 1905) just out of M.I.T., there was a place in American commerce for an innovator who could make a name for himself and become a top executive on the basis of his ability to design automobiles. But by 1925, individual effort seems to have lost its significance as large corporations swallow up smaller outfits like Dodsworth's own Revelation Automobile Company. Dodsworth no longer has a sense of purpose in his homeland and the possibilities for finding purpose in a defeated Europe do not seem great.

The dissatisfaction, the sense of being at loose ends, that afflicts Dodsworth throughout the novel is something he shares with most of Lewis's characters; except that there is something deeper, something more serious about Dodsworth's dissatisfaction. It borders on despair. Carol is dissatisfied with the possibilities for human fulfillment in the small town. Babbitt fails to find sufficient satisfaction in the business arena of Zenith. Arrowsmith is frustrated again and again in his search for truth. Ralph Prescott goes to the woods to avoid a case of urban neurosis. And even Elmer Gantry has his moments of hesitation when he thinks he should have

been a lawyer or should have remained a farm-implement salesman. Dodsworth's characterization combines aspects of Carol (her continual self-examination in relation to her discontent), Babbitt (his belief that despite his business successes and his realization of the middle-class dream, he should have done something else), and Arrowsmith (his inquisitiveness, his belief in the worth of individual inquiry and inventiveness, and his belief in the need for new ways of doing things). But Dodsworth goes beyond his fictional forebears in that his dissatisfaction is something that worldwide searching seems inadequate in alleviating. Like the later Hayden Chart and like Lewis himself, the dilemma is not simply a matter of dismal small towns, of a need for some entertainment that will provide the tired businessman with restful diversion, nor of a humanitarian desire to develop a new vaccine. It is a complex matter involving the coming together of personal and cultural crises.

In all of Lewis's major novels up to *Dodsworth* there is a steady movement toward the dead end; but only in *Dodsworth* is that dead end reached. Carol finds it possible to live in Gopher Prairie and shifts the responsibility for revolution onto her daughter. Babbitt, despite increased self-awareness, remains a Babbitt. Arrowsmith runs off to a new life and new freedom in the Vermont woods. And Elmer Gantry escapes (at least in this life) his day of judgment. But Dodsworth reaches a low point that is entirely his own among Lewis's heroes. He sits on his bed, alone in a Paris hotel, his wife off somewhere with her lover, and he is aware that he has become a drunk with nothing in the wide world to look forward to, nothing to do. He had been a pioneer, he had been a businessman, he had been a devoted family man, he had lived a distinctly American life, and it had led to a dead end. If he had a job, he would plunge into it for escape. If he had some friends handy, he would

run to them. But unlike Carol, Babbitt, Arrowsmith, and Elmer Gantry, he has no means of escaping from his crisis. He must look inward and find the source of his pain; then he must find a remedy. And in doing so, he becomes the first Lewis hero to go through a complete existential crisis (something Cass Timberlane and, to a degree, Kingsblood Royal in Lewis's later work were to experience).

We are made to see Dodsworth's personal crisis, however, as symbolic of the larger crisis his country is going through. Dodsworth is at once the pioneer and the businessman, a person of great energy and innocence with a strongly developed sense of right and wrong; he embodies those virtues that every American of his generation was supposed to have, the virtues that cleared the wilderness, settled the land, and won the war. But things had changed; the United States had become a corporate state, and there were new attitudes concerning the place of the individual in society, as well as a new morality to go along with those attitudes. Dodsworth realizes that he "could make no daring decisions for himself" after his company has merged with the United Automotive Company.

They had taken from him the pride in pioneering which was one of his props in life—and who *They* were he didn't quite know. *They* were something more than just Alec Kynance and a few other officers of the U.A.C. *They* were part of a booming industrial flood which was sweeping over him. . . . He had helped to build a machine which was running away from him.[28]

Adjustment to the new reality is no easy thing. Dodsworth "had no longer the dignity of a craftsman. He made nothing; he meant nothing; he was no longer Samuel Dodsworth, but merely part of a crowd vigorously pushing one another toward nowhere."[29] To a

large extent Dodsworth is a symbol of a national mood
that came out of the reaction to the sudden development
of the mass man. This mood was partly behind the hysteria of the 1920s and was reflected in the exhibitionism
found in the antics of the flapper and the improvisations
of the jazzman; the flapper's need to shock other people
with her behavior and the jazz musician's need to ad-lib
were both based on the deeper need to express individu-
ality. The mood of the 1920s was also expressed in ex-
patriatism; the hope that Europe, with its old-fashioned
ways, would provide escape from the horror of living in
the standardized American industrial state.

And Dodsworth foes find an escape of sorts. Europe gives him a sense of being distinct because he is
made aware, very quickly, that he does not fit in. He
becomes lonely and increasingly isolated from his wife,
who is trying, on the other hand, to become part of European society. He is forced to think about all of the
strangeness he confronts on his travels. He is forced to
make decisions while cut off from his friends, his family,
his job, and even his own language. This leads him to
that hotel room in Paris where he realizes he is alone
and at the end of things. But it also leads him toward
autonomy, a crucial and essential adjustment for indus-
trialized man to make, as David Riesman was later to
point out in *The Lonely Crowd* (an insightful analysis
of the social character of the middle-class urban American). As Dodsworth sees it, he has three choices. He
could adjust meekly to his culture and accept the narrow
range of choice it offers him; he could, as he says, sign
a contract with the United Automotive Company and
(even as a vice-president) be little more than an office
boy. He could choose rebelliousness and become a free-
spending, woman-chasing, boozehound like so many of
the men he meets on his travels. Or he could, as he eventually does, choose autonomy and make choices that

may or may not involve conformity, living the way his culture demands when it is beneficial to him that he do so and going outside cultural norms when there is advantage in it.

Lewis's novels all involve these choices, of course, with Carol choosing adjustment, Babbitt moving toward maladjustment, Arrowsmith wavering between maladjustment and autonomy, Elmer Gantry becoming negatively autonomous, and Dodsworth eventually attaining positive autonomy. Dodsworth can be trusted to use his autonomy well not only because of his essential goodness and his strong streak of traditional morality, but also because through his experiences in Europe, "He has gained aesthetic distance from his society; he is no longer immersed in it, and he no longer accepts its ways as given. He may or may not decide to obey any particular norm, for now he has freedom of choice."[30]

Dodsworth is the strongest of Lewis's moralities, and in it he presented a model for reform that has lasting implications in a world of Gross National Products and the omnipresent *They.* Dodsworth's plight and its resolution also have personal connotations for many readers. His crisis in middle age is one that has become common as many men at the height of their strength and abilities find themselves rendered useless by the corporation's thirst for younger blood, expanded operations, and greater profits through poorer-quality products. But what gives *Dodsworth* power as a social document is the way it responded to the peculiar crises of the 1920s as represented in Dodsworth himself. As Walter Lippmann has pointed out, "It so happened that the personal mood of Sinclair Lewis suited exactly the mood of a very large part of the American people. . . . *Main Street, Babbitt,* and, in a certain measure, *Arrowsmith,* became source books for the new prejudices and rubber stamps with which we of the Harding-Coolidge era examined ourselves."[31] *Dodsworth* is not a mere source-book, however; it, as are all of Lewis's novels to varying extents, is a guide book as well.

In his moral pronouncements directed toward the reform of the middle class in America, Lewis was distinctly a novelist of engagé, a term used to define a writer who is committed to social and political change. This fact has long had a negative influence on his reputation, despite the increasing irrelevancy of the new criticism with its disregard of background, statement, and social purpose in favor of structure and textual explication. But in the last ten years the validity of Lewis's kind of novel has returned, if indeed it ever was much out of fashion—in retrospect the method and results of Dos Passos, Steinbeck, and Mailer, whose books take us through the 1930s, 1940s, and 1950s, were not so much different from Lewis's. Truman Capote's *In Cold Blood,* Norman Mailer's *Why Are We in Vietnam?,* Mario Puzo's *The Godfather,* and Saul Bellow's *Mr. Sammler's Planet* are but a few of the many more-or-less best-selling novels that have conceptual bases close to *Main Street, Babbitt,* and the rest of Lewis's best-known books. Of course, the problem for all writers who involve themselves in the issues of their time and attempt to modify contemporary attitudes is that their themes and solutions may not be vital to the next generation of readers. But in the case of Lewis, he was so concerned with the fundamental problems of his culture that it is difficult to conceive of him going out of date, even though some of his novels—*Elmer Gantry* is an example—are not as pertinent as they once were. It is likely that at least a few of Lewis's moralities for a new time will prove to be moralities for all time—or until the Gopher Prairies and the Zeniths are no longer to be recognized through the descriptions he gave them.

3

The Question of Art

A more profound writer would not have had so assured a success; a less skillful one would not have been so influential in his success. But Lewis hit a certain average in art perfectly, as he hit off the native average—or what Americans like to think is the native average—so well in his characters; and that was at once his advantage and his misfortune.

—Alfred Kazin, *On Native Grounds*

Sinclair Lewis's novels have long been castigated for their inartistic qualities. Mark Schorer's pronouncement that Lewis was one of our "worst writers"[1] is the most famous comment on the aesthetic level of Lewis's work. But many other critics have also remarked on Lewis's deficiencies as a novelist. Mencken, for instance, in a review of *Main Street* that is otherwise full of praise, complained, "The figures often remain in the flat; the author is quite unable to get the poignancy into them which Dreiser manages so superbly; one seldom sees into them very deeply or feels with them very keenly."[2] Sherwood Anderson objected to Lewis's style: "The texture of the prose written by Mr. Lewis gives me but faint joy. . . ."[3] T. K. Whipple, in an article that is very sympathetic to Lewis, nonetheless saw Anderson as the better writer: "The very mention of Anderson brings into sharp relief Lewis's limitations—his superficiality, his meretricious writing, his lack of passion and of thoughtfulness."[4] Robert Cantwell called Lewis "one of the most plunging and erratic writers in our literary history; unpredictability, waywardness, unevenness are his distinguishing characteristics," and wrote that Lewis has "turned out as much journalistic rubbish as any good novelist has signed his name to, and he has written novels so shallow and dull they would have wrecked any reputation except his own."[5] Such citations from Lewis's critics could be repeated almost indefinitely because Lewis has been one of the most thoroughly castigated authors in American literature. But there is something about his writing that leads the reader, while at once agreeing with most of the attacks on Lewis's characterization, style, story sense, and inconsistency, to harbor at the same time a contrary feeling that much of the criticism is somehow unfair.

Certainly there is much that is irritating in most of Lewis's novels. His treatment of children and the way he had them talk is exceedingly cloying. Hugh's desire "to know what the box-elder tree said, and what the Ford garage said, and what the big cloud said"[6] in *Main Street* makes him sound like no son of Will Kennicott's. And Carol's conversation with Hugh is just as unrealistic and silly. When they are leaving Gopher Prairie on the train for Washington, Hugh asks Carol what a generation is; she replies, "It's a ray in the illumination of the spirit."[7] Such preciousness seems out of place in comparison to the authentic-sounding dialogue that runs through most of the novel (although there are plenty of passages in which Carol talks as if she were reading from *The Saturday Evening Post*).

Lewis's preciousness usually takes the form of overwriting, a bad habit he fell into during his long apprenticeship as a writer for popular magazines. The first description of Carol is an example: "A girl on a hilltop; credulous, plastic, young; drinking the air as she longed to drink life. The eternal aching comedy of expectant youth."[8] But it also is found in his occasional archaisms and syntactic inversions reminiscent of the watery Tennysonian verse he wrote as a college student (one has only to think of the descriptions of Babbitt's "fairy child": "warm ivory were her arms; and beyond perilous moors the brave sea glittered"[9]). In addition, as Rebecca West pointed out, there were problems in Lewis's word choice. He was, she said in reference to *Elmer Gantry,* "full of wilful abnegations of fine qualities. Why should Mr. Lewis, who used to tread the sward of our language as daintily as a cat, use the word *amour*? Not *an amour,* which is just good eighteenth-century English, but *amour.*" She cited the line, "When Elmer as a freshman just arrived from the pool halls and frame high school of Paris, Kansas, had begun to learn the decorum of amour." And then she added that it is "a loathsome usage. It makes one see a pimpled male child smoking a cheap cigar outside a place marked 'Eats,' sustaining his soul against the drabness of *Main Street* by turning over in his mind a nickelodeon conception of Europe."[10] Lewis wrote rapidly and nervously, so his weaknesses are not surprising; it is the suspicion of most readers regarding them, and it was Rebecca West's suspicion as well, that Lewis should have known better than to make the mistakes he did. He may not have been our worst writer but, given the stylistic excellence he attained at least once in all of his novels after 1920, his lapses make him appear to have been our most careless writer.

His best passages are almost always descriptive, and read in isolation, they provide a partial rebuttal to those who contend that Lewis's style is second-rate. The train ride the Kennicotts take when Carol goes to Gopher Prairie for the first time, the autumn countryside when Will takes Carol hunting, Zenith as Babbitt sees it on his way to work that first morning, Arrowsmith's sojourn in Wheatsylvania (another version of *Main Street,* perhaps superior in its spareness to the original), and the opening pages of *Elmer Gantry* with the terse foreshadowing implicit in the simple first sentence, "Elmer Gantry was drunk"—all of these passages are undeniable examples of good writing, and dozens more could be listed. But as photographic as Lewis's style is, he was also capable of suggestive sentences that give the lie to the notion that he was incapable of "deep thought." Such a sentence is found in *World So Wide* in a passage where he answered the persistent question in all of his novels—what is an American?—better and more lyrically than he does anywhere else: "He [Hayden Chart] knew then that he was unalterably an American: he knew what a special and mystical experience it is, for the American never really emigrates but only travels; perhaps travels for two or three generations but at the end is still marked with the gaunt image of Tecumseh."[11] Lewis's style is undeniably excellent in so many instances; but his lapses are in just about as many instances undeniably bad. And here again we come to the central problem in reading him: if he can be so good on page ten, how can he be so bad on page twelve?

Lewis, of course, is read and deserves to be read despite his sometimes unnerving inconsistency; but in trying to see his accomplishment for what it is, his own conception of style should be given some consideration. " 'Style,' " he wrote in the early 1930s, "is the manner in which a person expresses what he feels. It is dependent on two things: his ability to feel, and his possession, through reading or conversation, of a vocabulary adequate to express his feeling."[12] What is it that Lewis felt? Most of the people who knew him well observed that he was moved emotionally by two contrary influences: the romance of the past (Arthurian tales, the world of Scott and Tennyson, as well as a longing for a golden childhood) and the fascination in the clattering, kitsch-filled America of the 1920s. Sheldon Grebstein, in his study of Lewis, entitled the first chapter "The Two Sinclair Lewises," and there he made the point that Lewis as a writer "was constantly at war with himself. His novels are almost equally divided, each novel combining in itself these apparently hostile elements: half, the product of Lewis the satirist and realist; half, the work of the romancer and yea-sayer."[13]

This division explains much of Lewis's up-and-down quality. When reacting as a satirist, Lewis had an ability to feel that he could express effectively; his romantic impulses, however, were denied effective expression because he could not find an adequate vocabulary and was forced to fall back on the obsolete manner of the Victorian poets and novelists he had read as a boy. But when he reacted to chautauqua week in Sauk Centre, a realtors' convention in Minneapolis, or a throng of repenting sinners in a gospel tabernacle, he found the words he needed. Lewis the romancer was not completely denied, however; the many train scenes he has in his novels, the sunsets on the prairie, and the landscape of Europe in *Dodsworth* are evidence enough that Lewis's softer side did find occasional expression.

Lewis's great strength as a satirist was his ability to capture and mimic the rhetoric of the middle-class people his character were patterned on. But what is unmentioned in most discussions of Lewis as a mimic is the way he imitated other writers. At first, as in the Wells imitation of *Our Mr. Wrenn* and the Dreiser overtones in *The Job,* Lewis's mimicry seemed to be the traditional parroting of older writers by a younger. But in Lewis's 1920s novels are some passages that suggest Lewis was writing more than imitations; it is as if he were answering those critics who very early began the practice of comparing him unfavorably to other writers. Sherwood Anderson is the contemporary whose name most often comes up in these discussions, and it is thus surprising that so few critics have noticed the Vida Sherwin story in *Main Street,* a story that could very easily be inserted into *Winesburg, Ohio.* In giving us an account of Vida the schoolteacher's past and describing her secret passion for Will, Lewis provided the sort of psychological study of sexual repression that Anderson is noted for. Even the style of the Vida Sherwin section (chapter twenty-one) is like Anderson. Here, for example, is how the story begins: "Gray steel that seems unmoving because it spins so fast in the balanced flywheel, gray snow in an avenue of elms, gray dawn with the sun behind it—this was the gray of Vida Sherwin's life at thirty-six."[14] The story of Zilla Riesling in *Babbitt* is another tale in the mode of Anderson, but it is not as compressed and does not seem to be so immediately derivative.

Lewis's imitations—perhaps rebuttals or challenges would be better terms—are not confined to Anderson. One is forced by the subject matter of *Mantrap,* a trip into the Canadian wilds for the sake of renewal, to think of Hemingway's Michigan woods stories. And the theme of the American in Europe, upon which the plot of *Dodsworth* is based, is suggestive of Henry James. Indeed, one has the impression while reading *Dodsworth,* which differs significantly in tone and pace from anything else by Lewis, that Lewis wrote it to demonstrate that he was capable of writing a novel in the Jamesian manner.

The name of James is associated with the art of the novel, whereas the word "art" is used very little by most writers in commenting on Lewis. Henry James is the master, while Lewis is scarcely regarded as a craftsman. It is difficult to overpraise James, but in the case of Lewis and his ability to put a novel together, there has been a certain amount of underappreciation. His 1920s novels are cases in point.

Main Street is structured on the principle of contrast and virtually every chapter has its counterpoint.
This can be seen most directly, if not most dramatically,
in the back-to-back scenes contrasting Carol's first walk
down Main Street and the servant girl Bea Sorenson's
first impression of Gopher Prairie. The same technique
is used again and again—the contrast between the ugli-
ness of the town and the beauty of the prairie; between
the elaborate preparations behind Carol's Chinese party
and the short, matter-of-fact account of the party in the
local newspaper; the contrast between the scenes show-
ing Will as a dull husband and the scenes in which he is
depicted as a heroic small-town physician; and the cross-
country comparison of Gopher Prairie to Washington,
D. C. Contrast was used by Lewis within scenes as well
as in the broader comparisons that stretch across chapters. He cut back and forth from character to character,
usually using Carol as the reference point—Will's opinion of Rauskukle, the tycoon of New Wurtemberg,
against Carol's doubts concerning Rauskukle's value to
the community; Miles Bjornstam's socialism against
Carol's basic faith in capitalism; and Vida's belief in pa-
tient work to attain needed improvements against
Carol's persistent attempts to storm the citadels of the
establishment.

Contrast was also used to provide the reader with
a fuller conception of many characters in the novel. The
romantic appeal Guy Pollock has for Carol is dimmed
when he is seen sitting in the dusty shabbiness of his office. And the similar appeal of Erik Valborg, the tailor
with whom Carol has a brief romantic involvement, is
devastated when he is seen as a bit player in a second-
rate movie. In addition, Lewis employed the more subtle
kind of contrast implicit in the opening sentences of the
novel. Carol is standing on a hill where Indians had

camped only two generations before, but she is thinking of contemporary things—Brieux, hair styles, and her chemistry instructor. She is not aware of the short history of white man's civilization in Minnesota; and her lack of historical perspective shows again and again as she confronts the pioneer mentality of Gopher Prairie. Like all the varieties of contrast in *Main Street,* the first few sentences lead the reader into the point-counterpoint framework of the novel.

Lewis's symbolism develops out of this principle of contrast. Will, for instance, uses photographs of Gopher Prairie to induce Carol to marry him and live in the prairie town. Near the end of the novel, when he journeys to Washington to court Carol once more, Will again shows her some pictures of Gopher Prairie. The two sets of photographs are much alike. The first set is "streaky; she saw only trees, shrubbery, a porch indistinct in leafy shadows."[15] When she looks at the second set, she sees "the sun-speckled ferns among birches on the shore of Minniemashie, wind-rippled miles of wheat, the porch of their own house where Hugh had played. . . ."[16] Will has to comment on the first set; when he shows her the second set, he says nothing— Carol can interpret them on her own. What were once only shrubbery and trees have become ferns and birches; and what was once only an indistinct porch is her own house and the home of her child. Just as the photographs have become more distinct and meaningful to her, Gopher Prairie is seen with clarity by the end of the novel. Will's camera technique has improved and Carol's ability to understand the town has also improved. Lewis used the camera-eye technique throughout the novel to give the reader a picture of life in a small town; it is thus fitting that he should have used photographs to suggest what happens to Carol's perspective by the end of the

book. Like a good photographer, contrast was upper-
most with Lewis.

At first, *Babbitt* seems to be more of the same
thing. Babbitt's erotic dream about the fairy child that
opens the novel is contrasted with Babbitt's mundane
awakening and the accompanying washing and shaving.
But soon we are drawn into a more subtle kind of contrast, a contrast between the matter-of-fact, everyday
business world that dominates Babbitt's life and the
nightmarish quality given to the description of what
happens to him in that world. It is on this matter that
one must take issue with the conception of Lewis as a
photographic realist. To be certain, Lewis did capture
in a documentary way the life of a representative American businessman in the booming financial situation of
the early 1920s. But so many of the descriptive passages
in *Babbitt* are not realistic in the ordinary sense. Lewis's
choice of words, the way he described movement, and
the very sound of his language, make much of the novel
surreal. This is especially true when we see things
through Babbitt's eyes, as in the mist scene of chapter
twenty-three when Babbitt, overcome with ennui on an
autumn evening, goes for a walk and encounters in "a
chaos without turmoil or desire" a friend in an un-
guarded moment.

Through the mist came a man at so feverish a pace that he
seemed to dance with fury as he entered the orb of glow
from a street lamp. At each step he brandished his stick and
brought it down with a crash. His glasses on their broad
pretentious ribbon banged against his stomach. Babbitt in-
credulously saw that it was Chum Frink.[17]

The furious dance, the crashing stick, and the
banging of glasses of Chum Frink, a doggerel-writing
poet, give this scene a nightmarish aspect. And the many

scenes like it (Babbitt getting drunk at Tanis Judique's party, the coal-dealer and fellow-businessman Vergil Gunch shadowing the parlor-socialist Babbitt, the strike scene in chapter twenty-seven) make Babbitt's life seem more like a bad dream than anything else, his world the terrain of the subconscious, and his story almost like a descent into hell. Maxwell Geismer has elaborated on this last point, terming *Babbitt* "our native *Inferno* of the mechanized hinterland."[18] In *Main Street* Lewis gave us the thoughts of Carol Kennicott in a straightforward way; in *Babbitt* the nonverbal, deeply felt but ill-defined level of the hero's consciousness is much more a crucial part of the novel's structure.

Lewis cuts back and forth from the external Babbitt to the internal Babbitt, and as he does so, Babbitt emerges as a person who eventually engages the reader's sympathies. The novel begins with the external, with a description of Babbitt's city, Zenith. Then Lewis makes an abrupt shift into Babbitt's dream life, the kind of shift that occurs repeatedly in the novel, a shift from outer appearances to internal reality. Babbitt's dream, in contrast to the shining newness of Zenith, is an old one, an archetypal one. He dreams of a girl who is "so slim, so white," who waits for him "in the darkness beyond mysterious groves,"[19] who will sail away with him. She seems a combination of Eve, the Lorelei, Beatrice, and an underweight Gibson Girl. It is significant that Babbitt, whose name has come to stand for a life controlled by an obsession for conspicuous consumption and drowned in materialism, does not dream of houses or cars or cases of Canadian whiskey, but instead lies, like an overstuffed Shelley, on his narrow sleeping-porch bed and fills his brain with images of ethereal femininity and mysterious groves. This is the side of Babbitt we encounter first in the novel; the standardized Babbitt soon takes over, and we see him awakening, washing, talking to his family, driving to work, and going about his daily life.

It is to the internal Babbitt, however, that Lewis returns for the kind of development that takes place in the novel, for it is what the slim, white girl represents—companionship, escape to a kinder world, and sexual release—that determines Babbitt's story. So we see him faced with a series of psychological crises when he loses the companionship of Paul Riesling, when he finds that the Maine wilderness offers no satisfying alternative for the twentieth-century city dweller, and when he realizes that the eternal virgin who lurks in his racial unconscious is not to be found in an affair with a middle-aged widow. With each succeeding crisis, Babbitt grows more desperate, more discontented, to the point that he almost becomes a socialist, hovering on the brink of committing himself to destruction of the economic system that offers him so little possibility for happiness and heroism. In Babbitt's nervous dabbling in leftist causes can be seen the relentless romanticism that lies beneath the businessman's respectable appearance; and he almost becomes involved in revolution, the ultimate romantic act.

But the internal Babbitt, the Babbitt of brotherly love, of escape to the wilderness, free love, and revolution, is brought under control. The Good Citizens League pays him a visit, and he realizes how almost impossible it is for him to remain a renegade. He finds himself pressured by his wife to conform, ignored by his friends, and threatened with ruin in his business. If he is to continue to fight he would be certain to lose. Babbitt tries to think all of this out, but it is not until his wife is stricken with appendicitis and taken to the hospital for surgery that Babbitt makes an abrupt renunci-

ation of his freedom. The hospital scene is the most ter-
rifying moment in the nightmare of Babbitt's life, and
the description of that scene indicates the depth of horror in Babbitt's mind. Babbitt is sitting in the hospital
laboratory where

he was conscious only of a decayed object preserved in a
bottle of yellowing alcohol. It made him very sick, but he
could not take his eyes from it. He was more aware of it
than of waiting. His mind floated in abeyance, coming back
always to that horrible bottle. To escape it he opened the
door to the right, hoping to find a sane and businesslike
office. He realized that he was looking into the operating
room; in one glance he took in Dr. Dilling, strange in white
gown and bandaged head, bending over the steel table with
its screws and wheels, then nurses holding basins and cotton
sponges, and a swathed thing, just a lifeless chin and a
mound of white in the midst of which was a square of sal-
low flesh with a gash a little bloody at the edges, protrud-
ing from the gash a cluster of forceps like clinging para-
sites.[20]

The repetition of the word *white* reminds one of
Babbitt's dream world and the slim white girl, who, because of the brutality of Babbitt's waking world, has
become reduced to something like the pickled object in
the laboratory jar. Babbitt has lost his vision of beatitude.
On turning from his vision of the good and the beautiful,
he opens the door of what he thinks is an office. But instead of the order and security he had hoped for, he sees
a horrible collection of images—screws, wheels, basins,
and the reduction of the human form to a package of
meat on which operations are performed.

Dr. Dilling (the pickler) and the forces of conformity he represents have removed the fairy girl just as
efficiently as Mrs. Babbitt's appendix has been snipped
out. It is as if Babbitt has been lobotomized; he returns

to the laboratory and swears "faith to his wife . . . to Zenith . . . to business efficiency . . . to the Boosters' Club . . . to every faith of the Clan of Good Fellows."[21] He has had enough; he has seen his life for what it is, and he does not want to look anymore. The dream girl is gone, and Babbitt admits: "They've licked me; licked me to a finish."[22] And like that of Carol Kennicott, his story ends with a statement of hopefulness for the next generation, but little hope for himself.

The story of Babbitt is the story of the death of the romantic impulse in the twentieth-century world of business. *Arrowsmith,* in contrast, is the story of the survival of the romantic impulse in the twentieth-century world of science. Martin Arrowsmith is dark and mysterious looking, a truth seeker whose fight against disease and commercialism makes him an unusual character for the Lewis of the 1920s to have taken up. Reviewers were quick to notice a new Lewis in *Arrowsmith,* a more artistic, idealistic Lewis, who had discovered the potential for heroic action in the modern age.

At first, *Arrowsmith* seems to be a step forward for Lewis as a novelist. It is doubtful that Arrowsmith is any more firmly realized as a character than is Carol or Babbitt. Nor are the secondary characters in *Arrowsmith*—Max Gottlieb; Arrowsmith's first wife, Leora; Arrowsmith's medical-school friend Clif Clawson; and Almus Pickerbaugh, the Iowa health officer—developed any better than their counterparts in the two previous novels. But the story moves along faster and more surely in *Arrowsmith* as opposed to the relatively static quality of *Main Street* and *Babbitt.* The beginning of the novel, in which Arrowsmith's pioneer great-grandmother is depicted refusing to abandon her family's westward trek in the Ohio wilderness, corresponds nicely to the end, when Arrowsmith refuses to give up his search for truth.

And Lewis's handling of the scientific concepts and information necessary to give authenticity to his account of Arrowsmith's career as a physician and a bacteriologist is clear without being overly simplistic. He had considerable help of course, from Paul De Kruif, a Ph.D. in bacteriology, a researcher at the Rockefeller Institute, and later a successful writer of popular books on scientific topics. But despite the great contribution De Kruif made to the technical information in the novel, it was Lewis's skill in blending the narrative and the scientific detail so that the reader is not put off by lengthy explanations of complicated laboratory procedures that makes the novel readable.

In most respects, *Arrowsmith* displays Lewis's ability as a writer of the research novel better than any of his other books. All of Lewis's novels, with the exception of *World So Wide,* developed out of the notebook he devoted to his investigations of American life. In *Arrowsmith* his mastery of his subject matter is displayed as it is nowhere else, mainly because he achieved verisimilitude in describing scenes that are ordinarily comprehensible only to specialists such as De Kruif himself. The topics of his other novels—small-town life, real-estate selling, preaching, social work, hotelkeeping, acting—are not the mysteries to the general reader that the work of the scientist is. Thus, the strongest point that can be made about Lewis's artistry in *Arrowsmith* is that he takes the reader into the laboratory without boring him. This is no easy thing to do and the majority of novelists get around the problem simply by ignoring it, by telling the results of the scientist-hero's work but not how it is done.

Lewis paid a price for the plot movement in *Arrowsmith,* however. Leora's death from smoking a contaminated cigarette while Arrowsmith is chasing another woman is melodramatic and contrived; but if nothing else it speeds up Lewis's story. The entire scene on the island of Saint Hubert, when Arrowsmith tests his bacteriophage on the plague-ridden natives and then, in his grief over Leora, abandons the control he sets up for his experiment, is false as a crisis. Many commentators have pointed out that controls in such a situation would be unnecessary in the first place. If a high percentage of those inoculated survived the plague, the success of Arrowsmith's work would have been apparent, especially if a high percentage of those who resisted inoculation died. It is when Lewis gets Arrowsmith to Saint Hubert that his plot as well as his understanding of scientific method disintegrate.

Main Street and *Babbitt* lack such a moment of overly contrived drama and tension, and consequently they are better novels. *Arrowsmith* is more exciting, but in the same way that *Battle Cry* is more exciting than *The Naked and the Dead. Main Street* and *Babbitt* were written with a kind of restraint in plot development that make them more than simply popular novels; *Arrowsmith* is a popular novel and in retrospect seems to be the weakest of the five big novels Lewis wrote during the 1920s. Lewis was offered the Pulitzer Prize for the novel, but he refused it, partly on the grounds that he should have received it for *Main Street*. He was right.

Little can be said in defense of the way *Mantrap* was written other than that the characterization of E. Wesson Woodbury, the would-be sportsman, is amusing and memorable. Ralph Prescott, the hero, talks like a prig, and Alverna, the love interest, behaves like a goddess of the woods one moment and a manicurist the next. Lewis finished the novel in a hurry and one reason for its inadequacy is that he no doubt was looking ahead to *Elmer Gantry* while he was writing it.

In his review of *Elmer Gantry,* Krutch in a single sentence summarized most of the critical reactions that the novel elicited then and since:

Elmer Gantry, with its innumerable incidents and its many ramifications, is indeed a structure far more impressive than most satires, a sort of cathedral in which every stone is a gargoyle; and though there will be many who will not be able to read it without the Devil's question, "But what is art?" it is not likely that any review will answer that question definitively.[23]

Like *Babbitt, Gantry* is peopled with grotesques, Dickensian caricatures with names like Eddie Fislinger, Lulu Bains, Almon Jewings Strafe, and Mannie Silverhorn, all seen against a backdrop of such places as Gritzmacher Springs, Banjo Crossing, and Clontar. The way Lewis handled these bizarre characters and places is not essentially different from the way he handled the Chum Frink and the Galop de Vaches (the state capital of Winnemac) of *Babbitt.* What is different, however, is his treatment of the novel's central character, and it is to this that we must look in considering what Krutch called the devil's question of Lewis's art.

Elmer Gantry stands alone among Lewis's novels in that it does not progress toward a moment of self-awareness on the part of its central character. Carol Kennicott, George F. Babbitt, Martin Arrowsmith, and Ralph Prescott, as well as the later Sam Dodsworth, all have their moments of epiphany. But Elmer Gantry begins as a self-centered bully who "assumed that he was the center of the universe and that the rest of the system was valuable only as it afforded him help and pleasure,"[24] and he ends the same way, not much chastened by a blackmail attempt that nearly destroys his clerical career. Elmer's development is negative, and as his life

goes on he compounds a brand of grotesque folly and
evil that, quite conversely, makes him a more and more
successful clergyman. His story is the story of Mr. Bad-
man Making Good, a fable of deceit set against the
background of twentieth-century Christianity and sus-
tained through a high-pitched form of irony that makes
the abandonment of traditional plot structure (the movement toward self-discovery) possible. It is in *Elmer
Gantry* that Constance Rourke's conception of Lewis as a
fabulist[25] can be seen better than anywhere else, for the
novel drives inexorably, if not simply, toward an ironic
moral: "Dear Lord, thy work is but begun!"[26]

Lewis's mastery of irony is apparent throughout the
novel as well as in Elmer's final prayer. Virtually every
aspect of Elmer's personality and virtually every episode
in his life has its ironic counterpoint. Elmer's best ser-
mon has love as its theme, but Elmer cannot love anyone. Elmer is supposed to be a true believer, but he is in
fact little more than an agnostic (although he retains a
childlike suspicion that some of the beliefs he preaches
might be true). Elmer gains everything from his involvement with the church except what it is supposed to give
him—decency. One-by-one (and sometimes in twos and
threes) he violates each of the Ten Commandments (except the injunction not to kill, although it is uncertain
that he will avoid breaking it, at least indirectly, when
Napap is fully organized for the elimination of those
who harden their hearts to moral rearmament). And he
is called upon to play, usually in an inverted way, the
role of hero in Lewis's version of the shepherd and the
lost sheep, the prodigal son, the parable of the talents,
and the story of Job. Such a compilation of ironic traits
and incidents have, naturally enough, led to the assump-
tion that there is little good in Elmer Gantry and that
what Lewis achieved in the novel is a powerful indict-

ment of a religion that has sold itself out to the values of business and salesmanship.

But the page-by-page irony in *Elmer Gantry* adds up to more than simply an indictment of Christianity. The twentieth century has been depicted by many writers as an ironic age, an age in which things have been turned around—peace is waged, free love turns out to be very expensive, and businessmen "serve" their customers by selling goods at ever higher prices. It is a time when theologians argue that God is dead, and we are called upon to make existential commitments fully aware that all action is without ultimate value. In an age of contradiction, who is better prepared to be priest than *Elmer Gantry*? His life is fraught with irony and every word he preaches is ironic; yet he is what his congregation needs, wants, and gets.

It is perhaps the growing sense of irony that now makes one sympathize more with Elmer and almost like him in a way that was much more difficult for the reader in 1927. When *Elmer Gantry* was published, the Ginger Man, the Flimflam Man, and the Man with No Name were not around, and Herman Melville's Confidence Man had not been generally rediscovered. The notion of the antihero was not much in the minds of critics and certainly had not gained much public acceptance. That Elmer was thought of as a character beyond sympathy is not surprising, but we might now be surprised that Elmer does not turn out any worse than he does. Given a world in which he must make most of his choices with insufficient information and with no conception of consequences, it is startling that Elmer can come across so often as a comic figure. Despite his greed and all of his raging sexuality, Elmer somehow wants to do good. He does not, however, want to sacrifice himself in the process, and he is thus no true imitator of Christ and no

Christian. He is an unfaithful servant, but there are
traces in him of Chaucer's monk; the flesh and the spirit
have battled in him and the flesh has won, but the spirit
is still there. We should be glad that Elmer does not lose
his pulpit at the end. It would be too insufficiently ironic
that he could be done in so easily by so obvious a charge
as alienation of the affections. The alienation Elmer and
most men must deal with in this century is of a much
more serious kind.

The plot of *Elmer Gantry,* like the plot of *Arrowsmith,* has weaknesses, however, that detract somewhat
from the effectiveness of Lewis's irony. This is particularly true at the end, and Alfred Harcourt, Lewis's publisher, tried to get Lewis to come up with a different con-
cluding crisis for Elmer to face. "We all agree you
should consider the badger game episode more carefully
and either change it or substitute something for it," Harcourt wrote to Lewis in December of 1926. "A girl
clever enough to get away with being his secretary and
unscrupulous enough to badger him would not devote so
much time to so unpromising a subject financially."[27]
Harcourt added that it is unlikely that Elmer would,
after so many philanderings, be so worldly unwise as to
write letters and be so caught by surprise. Even a simple
weighing of the amount of time, the cost of renting an
apartment, and the other expenses Hettie and her husband go through in trying to bilk Elmer, against the
amount of money they would be able to get from him,
reveals the unlikelihood that they would have under-
taken such a venture in the first place. Lewis, of course,
did not take Harcourt's advice and the novel is weaker
because of it.

The Man Who Knew Coolidge cannot be faulted
on the basis of its plot; it has almost no plot at all. But
many other faults have been found in it, and most re-

viewers and critics have dismissed it as a long-winded extrapolation of the internal monologues that take place in *Babbitt*. This is unfortunate, because in retrospect, after the assimilation of James Joyce's *Ulysses* and the reawakened appreciation of Robert Browning's dramatic monologues, *The Man Who Knew Coolidge* is more delightful than tiresome and often seems downright hilarious. It contains some of Lewis's best humorous writing, especially in the sections in which Lowell Schmaltz gives us "The Story by Mack McMack" (one of the best shaggy-dog stories ever written), talks about his wife ("Well, as I say, now that I've mastered psychoanalysis, I can see things was all wrong with Mame and me from the beginning"[28]), and tells us how close he actually came to meeting President Coolidge. What is wrong with the novel is that Lewis covered the same ground he did in *Babbitt,* and to his readers in the 1920s it was anticlimactic. But the readability of *The Man Who Knew Coolidge* and its representative qualities as a piece of pure Lewis are suggested by the frequency of its excerpted appearance in anthologies.

Although *Dodsworth,* the last novel of Lewis's great decade, has a businessman for a hero, there is little of the anticlimax about it. *Dodsworth* has come to be regarded as possibly Lewis's best-written novel, even if it lacks the historical significance that is likely to make *Main Street* and *Babbitt* more enduringly important.

The stronger aspects of Lewis's artistry are all present in *Dodsworth*. He used the technique of contrast, for example, with the same mastery as in *Main Street*. On the larger scale, there is the contrast between America and Europe; but on a smaller, more subtle scale there is the contrast between characters and even the contrast within individual characters. Sam's solid middle-class maturity is in contrast to Fran's childishness. Edith

Cortright's compassionate attitude toward Sam is in contrast to Fran's scornful attitude toward him. Alec Kynance's ruthlessness as a corporation president is in contrast to Sam's creative attitude toward the manufacture and sale of automobiles. And this sort of contrast runs from start to finish through the novel, with sets of characters serving as foils to either Sam or Fran. On a deeper level, Fran and Sam exist as contrasting personalities each within himself. Sam the self-confident engineer exists alongside Sam the timid and ineffectual husband. Fran the bitchy and immature wife exists alongside Fran the charming cocktail-party conversationalist. This ability to depict characters who are near contradictions unto themselves was one of Lewis's strongest, an ability that was earlier demonstrated in the characterization of Babbitt as romantic and realist.

Much of the irony in *Dodsworth* comes out of the levels of contrast that are set up. It is ironic that Sam Dodsworth, the American businessman, is capable of achieving a more honest kind of leisure, a more appreciative comprehension of art, and a more sophisticated understanding of love than are most of the European aristocrats and artists he meets. It is ironic that Sam, who goes to Europe with many apprehensions about the value of old-world culture, should become more Europeanized than Fran, who goes there with that purpose in mind (and it is a further point of irony that Sam's understanding of America should increase the more he is drawn into European modes of living). Contrast and irony, while they dominate the novel, are only the more obvious of its strengths.

Dodsworth has a quietness about it that Lewis's novels generally lack. This is not only because contrast and the resulting irony are comparatively subdued. The handling of the plot, the landscapes against which the story takes place, and the very texture of the prose itself all contribute to the underplayed quality of the book. The plot moves forward in a clearly defined, logically developed way, free of the contrived situations that are a problem in *Arrowsmith* and *Elmer Gantry*. Nor does the plot lead toward a moment of crashing conflict. Sam drifts away from his wife and toward a better understanding of himself without going through a highly dramatic, heartrending scene in which all the causes of his marital discord are brought out into the open. The habit of thoughtfulness that Sam gradually develops is reinforced by the beauty of the countryside and the peculiar quality of the cities in Lewis's descriptive passages. This power of description is present in the earlier novels, particularly in *Main Street,* but in *Dodsworth* it is accompanied by a studied carefulness combined with a love of scene that makes the novel read, in places, like an old-fashioned travel book. The travelogue sections gain much of their effectiveness from the flow of Lewis's language, which retains its customary jazzy quality, but is smoother over longer passages. It is difficult to account for such a change in Lewis's style without getting into a computerized study involving adverb counts and sentence length, but the reader senses the change nonetheless.

In terms of Lewis's own definition of style one might find some explanation for the superiority of *Dodsworth*. Style according to Lewis, it will be remembered, is dependent upon a writer's ability to feel and his corresponding ability to find language suitable for expressing that feeling. It seems that Lewis felt more powerfully about the subject matter of *Dodsworth* than he did about the subject matter of any other of his big novels. "Of all Lewis's books *Dodsworth* is the most directly and deeply autobiographical," Grebstein wrote. "Its love story is es-

sentially Lewis's version of his marriage which ended in
divorce in 1927, and Fran is his depiction of Grace Hegger Lewis. We believe that the poignancy which distin-
guishes *Dodsworth* springs from this."[29] Lewis's first
marriage ended on the note of hesitancy that ends Sam
Dodsworth's; it apparently ended in sadness without the
shrill accusations that so often are a part of divorce. And
it is the absence of shrillness, of the overly charged rhetoric of loss, that makes the style of the novel right.
Lewis found the words he needed and the result is a
startling contrast to the noisiness of *The Man Who
Knew Coolidge*.

The treatment of love is one of the most difficult
problems for most novelists, and few are able to handle
it well. It is not a topic that one readily associates with
Lewis, but a reading of *Dodsworth* provides ample support for the position that in at least one novel he handled it extremely well. The story is not developed as a
simple situation involving a flirtatious wife and a well-
meaning husband. Fran is depicted in such a way that
we come to see why Sam is repelled by her yet cannot
stop loving her. At the same time we see that Sam, for
all of his steadfastness and morality, has not been a very
attentive husband. Fran is a frigid woman, but one is re-
minded of the continental axiom that there are no frigid
women, only inept men. Sam's success in the automotive
industry has been purchased in part through neglect of
his wife. And this sort of subtlety in characterization
gives us a perceptive and mature account of what love is
and how it fails. One of the many ironies about *Dodsworth* is that it should provide such an effective study of
love and yet be written by a man who had so much difficulty loving and being loved. But then there is an essential inconsistency in both Lewis's life and work that
makes categorizing his writing very difficult.

The easiest way to understand Lewis's artistry is to think of him simply as a master of the popular novel. "Lewis knew the ingredients for writing for this new popular audience of the 1920's," Robert L. Coard pointed out in a perceptive study of *Dodsworth*: "a controversial topic; a contemporary setting; lots of accurately observed details; a clear plot; broad contrasts of characters, ideas, and languages; plenty of eye breaks in chapters and paragraphs and sentences; plenty of sentences strongly phrased and climactically located."[30] His control over such elements of technique was no slight accomplishment; and it undoubtedly accounted for the huge number of devoted readers Lewis enjoyed in his heyday, readers who remained surprisingly loyal to him through the weaker, although still controversial, novels he wrote during the 1930s and 1940s.

But there is a level of accomplishment in Lewis's five major novels that cannot be explained in terms of the way he used the tools of his trade as a popular novelist (although it must be remembered that he, more than any other twentieth-century novelist, is responsible for developing those tools). He conceived heroes who became essential reference points for students of American culture. He wrote at least four novels (*Main Street, Babbitt, Arrowsmith,* and *Elmer Gantry*) that are *tours de force* and that have not been outclassed by any subsequent novels on the same topics. He successfully responded to and caught the mood of his times, a point that is underscored by the first Mrs. Lewis who asks and answers: "Were the 1920's really the Jazz Age except for a few? Most Americans at that time lived more like Sinclair Lewis characters; there was more substance to life than Fitzgerald's glossy version."[31] Our idea of the 1920s as an era is likely to be influenced by Lewis's depiction of it for a long time to come. And the range of

his interest, the primal quality of his imagination, and
the sense of plight that is pervasive in his writing, all in
combination with a style that however erratic nonetheless fits the clattering internal-combustion society he de-
scribes, add up to an achievement that demands, yet de-
fies, appreciation. Perhaps the best way of all to deal
with Sinclair Lewis is to think of him as a one-man
Sturm und Drang movement; such a conception would
at least allow for a justification, in terms of art, of the
strong nationalistic and folk element, the adolescent fer-
vor, the restlessness, the agony of repressed passion and
the spiritual struggles in his writing. It would also enable
one to accept a critical fact about Lewis that might
otherwise be difficult to swallow; that he is a law unto
himself.

4

The Essayist

If anybody wants an article from me and wants to pay 75 cents a word, I may, and may not, be interested.
—Sinclair Lewis, Letter to John D. Chase

Sinclair Lewis's great popularity as a writer did not make him a literary dictator, but it did establish a market for his opinions. Shortly after the publication of *Main Street,* newspapers and magazines began besieging him for articles, book reviews, autobiographical information, and even accounts of his perpetual travels. And Lewis responded with a generous amount of nonfiction, most of which has remained uncollected and has received little attention since his death. This part of Lewis's work is worth consideration not only for the light it throws on his novels, but also for its own sake.

Lewis was an essayist of considerable power and skill, and for over thirty years his commentaries on books, events, and places appeared often in *The Nation, The Saturday Review of Literature, The American Mercury,* and, later, in *Esquire.* A detailed study of Lewis the essayist would constitute a book in itself and the number of chapters, given the variety of topics on which he wrote, would be large. But a brief overview of Lewis the essayist is nonetheless of value simply because it serves to reveal, in outline, a side of Lewis's artistry and personality that has been too much neglected.

As might be expected, one of Lewis's persistent concerns as an essayist is the role of the writer in American society. He deals with this topic most prominently and most successfully in his famous Nobel Prize address, "The American Fear of Literature," but he anticipated the remarks in that speech several times in earlier pieces. "Self-Conscious America," written for the October 1925 issue of the *American Mercury,* for example, should be

read in conjunction with "The American Fear of Literature." In "Self-Conscious America" Lewis pointed out
that art in America seems to be justified only if it is
"Doing Something Worth While."[1] The American writer
is supposed to operate out of a sense of duty, going
about his work not because he likes it, but because it is
something he is expected to do if he is to be honest or
respectable. He is also to align himself with a particular
attitude toward writing, to choose between the avant-
garde (imitating Joyce, Stein, Pound, and Proust) and
the other extreme, the "popular" (Mary Roberts Rine-
hart, Irv Cobb, and Pete Kyne). The dilemma of the
American writer is that he is pressured too strongly "to
choose between literary baseball fans and the Boy
Scouts of Dadaism."[2]

American writers are supposed to be self-conscious
as a civic duty, said Lewis; and when they go to Europe
and hang around with the other expatriates at the Café
Dôme, they become even more self-conscious, finding it
necessary to claim that they are in Europe to better
understand the United States, not simply because France
is an enjoyable place to be. "Solemnly to counsel authors that they may write as they wish seems as puerile
and platitudinous and absurd as to quote 'Honesty is the
policy,' " emphasized Lewis. "But in a country where
every one from the newest reporter on the Kalamazoo
newspapers to the most venerable professors at Harvard
. . . is replete with holy arms for all contemporary authors, there is no gospel more novel—or repulsive to
Americans, the most self-conscious and exaggerated
people in the world."[3] Lewis's conviction that the greatest problem American writers face is to find the courage
to "write as they wish" is echoed in another article,
"Can an Artist Live in America?" which appeared in
The Nation of 9 December 1925. Lewis ridiculed the

question contained in the title, pointing out that a writer can live anywhere, and then listed successful writers who have gone abroad and others who have stayed home, ending with this advice to young authors: "Do what you want to . . . if you can."[4]

The central thesis in "The American Fear of Literature," the speech Lewis delivered before the Swedish Academy in Stockholm on 12 December 1930, is a development of his objection to the idea that the American writer is supposed to be doing what is generally considered worthwhile—something that will be a credit to the country. Americans, according to Lewis, fear literature that does not glorify the United States. Writers consequently must resist coercion on all sides if they are to write as they wish. Once again he returned to the essential American paradox—that the last thing to be found in America, the land of freedom, is freedom itself—that runs through his fiction. American writers are free to praise, but not to blame; free to write in an "accepted" style, but not necessarily in the style that is best for them. And even when a writer starts out with a determination to tell the truth, as Hamlin Garland did, he is steadily beaten down until he is tamed. "And it is his tragedy, it is a completely revelatory American tragedy," Lewis stated, "that in our land of freedom, men like Garland, who first blast the roads to freedom, become themselves the most bound."[5] The American writer is thus forced into a defensive position, almost as if he is an enemy of the state. And to remain true to his art, he "must work alone, in confusion."[6]

The condition of the writer in America is, to a large extent, the result of the unwillingness to give up the pioneer mentality that seems to characterize American culture. This unwillingness was attacked again and again in Lewis's novels, and it came up for attack once more in the Nobel Prize speech. Lewis maintained that the most beloved writers in America are those who claim that the United States

is still as simple, as pastoral, as it was when it had forty million; that in an industrial plant with ten thousand employees, the relationship between the worker and the manager is still as neighborly and uncomplex as in a factory of 1840, with five employees . . . that, in fine, America has gone through the revolutionary change from rustic colony to world-empire without having in the least altered the bucolic and Puritanic simplicity of Uncle Sam.[7]

This national reluctance to face the realities of change is reinforced by the American universities in their hesitation to teach contemporary literature, by the American Academy of Arts and Letters in its ignorance of new artists, and by the new humanists (a conservative school of literary criticism) in their scorn for any literature but the most restrained. There is a divorce in America, Lewis contended, of intellectual life and "all authentic standards of importance and reality."[8]

But there is no shortage of younger writers who are willing to resist conformity and to write as they see fit, Lewis said, as he concluded the speech with praise of the younger generation. He mentioned Hemingway, Wolfe, Wilder, and Dos Passos as writers who were possibly to provide America with "a literature worthy of her vastness."[9] It was almost with some regret that he said he was too old to be considered one of them—regret that was needless because Lewis had already set them an example of the value of doing things one's own way.

Lewis was consistently sympathetic to younger writers and much of his essay writing consists of advice to them. "Self-Conscious America" and "Can an Artist Live in America?" were partly written to that purpose.

"The American Scene in Fiction," published in the New York *Herald Tribune* book section of 14 April 1929, reiterates much of the same advice that occurs in most of Lewis's pronouncements on what a writer should and should not do—be honest, pay close attention to his setting, and try to find his story material among the people and in the places he is most familiar with. Lewis was especially sympathetic to midwestern writers and went out of his way to encourage such writers from his own region as Frederick Manfred and August Derleth.

Lewis's readiness to accept other writers and his unusual lack of jealousy prevent his literary essays, consisting mainly of book reviews, from being much more than appreciations; but they are appreciations in the best sense of the word—the reactions of a careful reader to books he likes or thinks are important. A typical Lewisian review is the one he wrote of Henry S. Canby's *Age of Confidence* for the *Saturday Review of Literature* (6 October 1934). Canby's book is a personal account of Wilmington, Delaware, in the 1890s. "It is a refreshment to discover that not all of the American tradition is determined by P. T. Barnum and Huck Finn and Jim Hill," Lewis wrote in the positive manner that is part of his style as a reviewer, "but that also, for some hundred years there has been, in many Wilmingtons, a tradition of quiet civilization."[10] But Lewis was not hesitant to criticize harshly, as he demonstrated in the same essay when he takes time out to agree with Canby's negative review of John O'Hara's *Appointment in Samarra*: ". . . the erotic visions of a hobbledehoy behind the barn, even though the barn does figure in the novel as a 'country club.' "[11]

Lewis did a great deal of book-reviewing during his career as a writer and twice served as a regular reviewer for magazines. For a few months, beginning in October

1937, he did the "Book Week" section for *Newsweek*; and in 1945 he did a series of essay-reviews for *Esquire*.

Although he was a kindly critic, he was not reluctant to poke fun at some of the more prominent writers of the 1930s. In "Literary Felonies," a piece printed, as so many of Lewis's essays were, in the *Saturday Review of Literature* (3 October 1936), Lewis satirized Hemingway, Faulkner, and Dos Passos, among other writers, by imitating their quirks of style and plot. The Hemingway section is entitled "Obtaining Game under False Pretenses." Here is a sample:

By now the kudu was 516 meters away. I aimed pretty carefully. "You're a swell woodchuck killer!" jeered the L.L. I went on aiming. It was swell. I felt fine. The o.e. shouted, "It's certainly swell! I feel fine! You're a swell shot!" And maybe I was. . . . The kudu stopped and died. We all had a drink of beer. We felt fine.[12]

But as much book reviewing as Lewis did, and as much attention as he devoted to the condition of literature in the United States, his social criticism generally had more bite. Because of the nearly overwhelming sociological data in his novels, newspapers and magazines were eager to tap him for articles on "conditions" he observed as he traveled across the country and overseas. Lewis was not reluctant to take on these assignments and he wrote articles such as "I Return to America" for the *Nation* (4 June 1924), in which he analyzed the curious indifference of his countrymen toward politics even in an election year; "Publicity Gone Mad" for the *Nation* (6 March 1929), in which he objected to the increasing use of testimonials in advertising (saying that he has been asked to endorse various brands of pencils, radios, and breakfast food); and "Gentlemen, This Is Revolution" for *Esquire* (June 1945), in which he

warned of the coming cultural revolution of blacks in
America and of the nonwhite races of the world.

But the most moving and most memorable social
criticism written by Lewis is "Cheap and Contented Labor," a series of articles he did for the Scripps-Howard
newspapers in 1929 on the plight of the mill workers in
Marion, North Carolina. Lewis wrote with a fine sense
of outrage about the mood in a town where deputy sher-
iffs tried to break up a strike by firing upon the march-
ing workers, killing five and wounding more than
twenty. He described how the workers were being forced
to live in substandard housing, how they were the victims of the North Carolina legal system, and how some
of them, including Old Man Jonas, who struck a police
officer with his cane, were gunned down. He named
names, developed character sketches (of individual
strikers, of the county sheriff, of the judge who presided
at the grant jury hearing, and of the company president), and captured an atmosphere that is convincingly
real. It is newspaper writing that anticipated the best of
Jimmy Breslin in its taut simplicity and underlying
anger.

Lewis's style as an essayist is at its peak in his version of what happened in Marion. It is a style differing
from that of his fiction in giving an impression of tight-
ness and restraint that is often a stiff contrast to the more
freewheeling style of his novels. But Lewis did use many
of the same techniques in his nonfiction as he did in his
fiction. The long lists of objects, names, places, and
ideas that pile up in his novels are equally present in his
articles. The evidence of research, indicated by his com-
mand of the facts and his knowledge of other books on
the same topic when he was writing reviews, is also
there. And the Lewisian wit, which so often depends on
anticlimax, is abundant. Here, for example, is how he

characterized the typical 1920s expatriate: "Almost all the authors have written two or three devastating stories for the magazines which are printed on lovely, thick, creamy paper and which last, often, for five months, and one of them once bought a drink for a woman from his home town, and paid for it."[13]

Although Lewis's wit was often biting and his sentences under tight rein in most of his nonfiction writing, he often conveyed a mood of relaxation, especially in his autobiographical essays. These writings are not extensive, but in reading them, one is struck by the amount of self-awareness they reveal. Lewis's attitudes toward his life and his books in the few essays that comprise his memoirs are reasonable, refreshingly devoid of self-pity, and persuasively honest—something that is surprising to the reader who supposes that Lewis lived a life of self-deception.

Lewis's accounts of his younger days are particularly valuable not only for the details about his early career but also for the picture they present of the 1900–1920 era. "That Was New York and That Was Me," for example, an article published in *The New Yorker* of 2 January 1937, deals with Lewis's first day in New York, when he was en route to New Haven to begin his freshman year at Yale in 1903. He described disembarking from the Hudson River bay boat into smoky darkness, taking an erratic trolly journey to Grand Central Station, and suffering a kind of disillusionment from which he never recovered:

The golden streets of the dream city were not merely tarnished; they were greasy. Everywhere people bumped along the shadow-looking streets as viciously, as threateningly, as they had at the ferry house. Their eyes seemed full of a passion of malice and every manner of crime, and in their deft dodging at street corners, there was a surly, defiant,

urban competence which the young man from Minnesota
could surely never emulate.[14]

Another essay, "Two Yale Men in Utopia," printed
in the New York *Sun* of 16 December 1906, depicts Upton Sinclair's communal experiment at Helicon Hall in
New Jersey with the same vividness given to New York
City in 1903 (Lewis, it will be recalled, worked as a
furnace tender and janitor at Helicon Hall during November 1906). "This is certainly an intellectual joint,"
Lewis wrote. "This afternoon the cook, the scullion, the
chambermaid, and the Columbia instructor in philosophy got into a calorific discussion of the decadence of
George Moore, with sidelights on Max Nordau."[15] But
the most detailed and amusing account of happenings in
the first part of this century is to be found in a series of
articles that Lewis wrote for *Cosmopolitan* in 1947
about his days as a newspaper writer.

"I'm an Old Newspaperman Myself" is divided into
three sections—"Harry, the Demon Reporter," "You
Meet Such Interesting People," and "You Get around
So Much"—and takes Lewis from his first job (at no
pay) for the Sauk Centre *Weekly Herald* at the age of
fourteen through his later jobs with the Waterloo, Iowa,
Courier, and the San Francisco *Evening Bulletin.* Three
sections of these essays are particularly valuable in
understanding Lewis's youth and his own attitude toward it. The first is the account given of his adolescence
in Sauk Centre while he was working for the *Weekly
Herald* (and subsequently for the rival paper, *The Ava-
lanche*). Here, without apology and apparently without
regret, Lewis told how he was "a skinny, perpetually
complaining small boy"[16] who was consistently unable
to impress anyone in the gang of boys who tagged along
after his older brother Claude. It is essentially the same

story to be found in Mark Schorer's biography of Lewis, but Lewis's problems as a boy sound quite different when he pointed them out himself.

The second important segment of "I'm an Old Newspaperman Myself" is devoted to a recollection of Lewis's life at Carmel-by-the-Sea in California, where he worked as a part-time secretary to two now-forgotten writers, Grace Macgowan Cook and Alice Macgowan. His leisurely life in that land of abalone and muscatel is punctuated with an anecdote about Jack London reading Henry James's "sliding, slithering, glittering verbiage" aloud for the first time, banging the book (*The Wings of the Dove*) down on the table and wailing, " 'Do any of you know what all this junk is about?' "[17] But it is also punctuated with an afterthought in which Lewis had some doubts about his giving up that hand-to-mouth existence to become a respectable young book editor. "If I had had a few more drops of the tramp in me, like Hemingway or Poe," he wrote, "I might have become a great writer instead of a careful chronicler of domestic rows."[18]

The third memorable segment of the essays on Lewis's career as a journalist concerns his collaboration with a San Francisco hotelkeeper on a fake story about a bellhop who uncomplainingly waited on a cranky old lady who never tipped him. When the old lady died, she left the bellhop $20,000. "I made our Bobby Johnson so tender to his elders, so given to brushing his teeth and combing his hair and saving of electric light and pieces of string, that he was a model for all future youth," Lewis recalled. "Probably you can still see the influence of it, almost forty years later."[19] And then, in an aside that reveals much about the newspaper world of that day, Lewis mentioned that a few months later, when he had moved on to a job with the Associated Press, the hotelkeeper showed him a scrapbook full of clippings; the bellhop story had been picked up by papers throughout the United States and Europe.

But most direct statements of self-awareness by Lewis are found in a sketch that was apparently written for his German publisher sometime in 1927 and was discovered by the executors of the Lewis estate. This insightful self-portrait, which was published in *The Man from Main Street,* contains Lewis's own pronouncements on his talkativeness, his unappealing appearance, his lifelong ineptitude at games, his wide reading, his ability to work anywhere, his incessant traveling (a sign of his lack of imagination, he thought), and his contrary impulses toward romanticism and realism. In its quiet tone and convincing forthrightness, this essay does much to discount the popular notion of Sinclair Lewis as a deeply tortured, anxiety-ridden individual whose only recreations were the bottle or long sessions of feverish writing.

Another essay of somewhat the same kind is "The Death of Arrowsmith," a mock obituary published in the July 1941 issue of *Coronet*. In writing of his own death at the age of eighty-six, Lewis assessed his own accomplishments and failures. "Mr. Lewis seems essentially to have been a cheerful pathologist," he wrote, "exposing the clichés and sentimentalities of his day—the hearty falseness of senators and what were once known as 'business boosters,' the smirking attitudes toward women in his times, the personal ambitiousness of the clergy, the artists and the professional men, and the brazen mawkishness of patriotism."[20] He saw himself as a smiter of sentimentality, a stylist deriving from both Dickens and Swinburne (as well as from Wells, A. E. Housman, Thomas Hardy, H. L. Mencken, and Hamlin Garland), an experimental traveler, a mediocre actor (again with parallel to Dickens), and an eccentric "Last Surviving Connecticut Yankee."[21] Unlike Hemingway (who Lewis predicted would be killed leading Filipino and Chinese troops in 1949 during the final assault on Tokyo), Lewis did not see himself inspiring a school of imitators, although he surmised that his impact on American literature "has been healthful in his derision of dullness and formalism, his use of American lingo and humorous exaggeration intermingled with the more nearly scholastic manner that was an inheritance from his college days."[22] In this essay, as in much of the self-directed writing he did, Lewis was his own best critic and biographer.

Some of Lewis's essays, while partially autobiographical, are more on the order of reminiscences. One of the best of these is an article he wrote for *Good Housekeeping* in 1935, "This Golden Half-Century, 1885–1935." Lewis did not write directly about himself in assessing the developments since the time he was born, but he did write about what he had seen come to be in his lifetime—not only the inventions, but also the people and the events. He compared the fifty years between 1885 and 1935 with the previous half-century and was not altogether certain that the second fifty years had necessarily had the most genuine progress or the greatest men. What the essay amounts to is a remarkable history of an era by a man who had seen it all, had lived through it, and could honestly harbor neither hope nor despair concerning the future: ". . . just ahead of us may lie the world's most vicious war, or the benign curing of cancer and tuberculosis; another Shakespeare, or another scourge of Dillingers in low places and Kreugers in high; a flight to Mars, or a descent into an ocean of lava; a peaceful world nation, or a world shattered into ten thousand bandit tribes."[23]

Somewhat in the same mood are Lewis's travel writings, many of which are semi-Dodsworthian tours of England and the continent. Virtually every trip Lewis took across the Atlantic was accompanied by a request from an American newspaper to do a series of articles on his impressions of wherever he was traveling. He wrote, for instance, a number of articles called "Main Streets and Babbitts of Britain" for the New York *Herald Tribune* in 1928, which resulted from the wedding trip he took with Dorothy Thompson from London to Edinburgh and back by trailer, a then novel mode of traveling. But the best of his travel writing are those that deal with the United States, writings that are perhaps better termed "place studies." Two of these include pieces devoted to the two states he loved the most. "Minnesota, the Norse State," published in *The Nation* of 30 May 1923, is a portrait that was designed to correct eastern misconceptions of Lewis's native grounds. "Back to Vermont" was printed in the April 1936 issue of *The Forum* and is an enthusiastic explanation of why Lewis, the perpetual traveler who was more at home in a hotel room than anywhere else, was trying to put down roots (during the June to October season at any rate) on a farm in the Vermont hills.

These essays, along with others like them, are evidence of the strong sense of place Lewis demonstrated in his novels. Within a few days after arriving anywhere, Lewis would have inquired into the local history, interviewed his neighbors, and begun making comparisons to the other places he had similarly investigated. Had Lewis lived a century earlier, when the demand for travel books was larger, it is possible that his restlessness and his curiosity would have earned him a reputation in that genre.

But Lewis does deserve a considerable reputation

as an essayist—a reputation, however, that the notoriety of his novels will probably continue to obscure. He was all of the things a good esssayist should be—possessive of cutting wit, inquisitive, widely read and traveled, capable of righteous anger and gentle appreciation, and, above all, able to write in an entertaining way. Some of his essays contain his best writing and many of them reveal a side of his nature that is not so apparent to those who read only his novels; it is in his essays that his personality is most engagingly revealed and it is to them that we must turn to fill in our picture of the complete Lewis.

5

The Survivor

There was something meretricious about the ends of many of the talents of the time. . . . It made H. L. Mencken and any Rotarian brothers under the skin, men unfit to cope with the troubles that after 1929 buried both the graces and the faults of the twenties.

—Elizabeth Stevenson, *Babbitts and Bohemians*

"And nowadays, at forty-six, with my first authentic home—a farm in the pastoral state of Vermont—and a baby born in June, 1930, I am settled down to what I hope to be the beginning of a novelist's career. I hope the awkward apprenticeship with all its errors is nearly done!"[1] So Lewis wrote in the self-portrait he did for the Nobel Foundation, but what he hoped would be the beginning of his career as a writer is instead seen by most critics as the beginning of the end, for there is nothing in Lewis's writing after 1930 that matches the accomplishment found in *Main Street, Babbitt,* or even *The Man Who Knew Coolidge.* Lewis's later books all have their moments of brilliance, many of them are quite readable, several (*It Can't Happen Here* and *Kingsblood Royal*) were and still are relevant, and most of them turned a substantial profit for both author and publisher. But the novels of Lewis's last two decades share a common fault that makes it impossible for a reader to return to them with anything like the kind of enthusiasm his earlier work arouses: they fail to sustain mood, argument, and style, a failure that results in abrupt shifts from tough-minded realism to distressing sentimentality, radical social criticism to sympathetic treatment of reactionary ideas, and taut imagistic prose to strings of clichés and outdated rhetoric. Yet most of these novels were significant statements in their day, and all of them attest to a struggle for literary survival that

104

few other prominent writers of the 1920s were able to mount.

The weaknesses apparent in Lewis's writing during the 1930s and 1940s are all evident in the first novel he published during that era, *Ann Vickers,* which appeared in 1933. *Ann Vickers* is such an abrupt drop in quality from *Dodsworth* that one can only assume that winning the Nobel Prize must have made Lewis too self-conscious. He said as much himself as he was beginning to work on *Ann Vickers*: "It will presumably be published in the autumn of 1932, and the author's chief difficulty in composing it is that after having received the Nobel Prize, he longs to write better than he can!"[2] In all of Lewis's later novels there is a sense of struggle with style that indicates he was indeed trying to write on a level that was unnatural to him. The unfortunate result is that in attempting to write better than he could, he wrote worse.

Surprisingly, most reviewers praised *Ann Vickers* when it came out, almost as if they were pulling for the Nobel laureate not to falter. The book was published simultaneously in thirteen languages and eventually had a sale of over 130,000 copies, a total that was amazingly high for the Depression era. Many readers apparently warmed to and were shocked by the story of a midwestern girl who goes east to college early in the century, gets involved in the women's suffrage movement, becomes a social worker and eventually a successful penologist. The novel concentrates on the heroine's attempts at reforming American prisons, but the most sensational aspects of the novel are sexual. Ann has an abortion after an affair with an army officer named Lafayette Resnick, she later marries and separates from another man, and she ends by deciding to throw her lot in with a judge whose dealings get him into trouble with the law and whose child she decides to bear out of wedlock. This is strong stuff for the normally reticent Lewis, but his treatment of it is anything but erotic; it is merely topical.

The novel is, according to Schorer, a *Bildungsroman*; that is, it attempts to depict a period in history through the life of its central character as he comes into contact with culture and society.[3] The story begins about the same time as that of *Main Street* and is in effect a tracing of the growth of pre-World War I socialist idealism into its development as late-1920s, early-1930s liberalism. Inasmuch as this was achieved, the book provided Lewis with something of a transition piece into the Depression years when there was increased emphasis on social reform. But as important as the central concern of the book is, the theme of penal reform is dealt with in such a simplistic manner that the prison section becomes little more than an extension of the liberal cliché that holds that all prisoners are essentially good, that it is society that is at fault.

One wishes that Lewis's treatment of prison conditions were as vivid as the description he gave of labor conditions in the essay "Cheap and Contented Labor." But instead we get a southern prison, Copperhead Penitentiary, whose warden is Dr. Slenk (read Slink) and whose head guard is Cap'n Waldo, a sadistic archredneck. The prisoners are all unfairly imprisoned and the reader is invited to let his liberal heart bleed for them. It is, of course, true that prisons in Lewis's day were mismanaged (as they still are) and that many inmates were placed in prison for the wrong reason. But most people who work in penitentiaries quickly learn that while prisoners are not necessarily depraved, the majority do have some serious sociopathic condition in need of treatment. That Lewis did not realize this indicates that his research was not as thorough or as objective as it had been in his earlier books. And this is a general problem; in his post-1930 writing he seems to have become a lazier writer.

Lewis's position as a moralist in his 1920s novels contrasts greatly with the uncomplicated, shallow moral pronouncements that occur in *Ann Vickers*. His opinions on criminals and the legal system are an example. "There are no criminals and no prisoners," he wrote, "but only men who have done something that at the moment was regarded as breaking the law, and who at the hit-or-miss verdict of a judge (who was no judge at all, but only a man judging, in accordance as his digestion and his wife's nagging affected him) were carted off to a prison."[4] Does this mean that laws are bad, that there are no fair judges, that there are no men who are justly convicted of crimes? Lewis provided no answer other than an apparent and silly yes. His moral position in the novel is even more strange in the endorsement he gave to the Nietzschean theory of romance (superwoman needs superman), through which Ann justifies her affair with Barney Dolphin, the judge. He indicated, with no satirical intent, that the intellectual supremacy of Ann and Barney puts them above the restrictions of conventional morality; Ann is free to abandon her husband and Barney his wife with no guilt feelings. How unreal and shallow is such a version of love and marriage when compared to the sufferings of Sam and Fran Dodsworth.

Perhaps the love of Ann and Barney would be acceptable if Lewis had succeeded in developing them as superior persons (how a writer could do this is uncertain). But neither one is convincing. Barney is a handsome judge who is unable to conceal his conflicts of interest. And Ann comes across at best as half-educated, the sad type of liberal American woman who is obsessed with reforming society but does not understand enough about it to even know where or how to begin. She is not even convincing as a woman: she is Lewis imagining, not knowing, how a cultured woman thinks and acts.

The novel has many other weaknesses, most of which are evident enough. It begins with a scene out of Ann's childhood, a scene that is a weakness in itself because Lewis was never able to depict children without being overly sentimental. It ends without the character- istic and effective ambiguity that always makes the reader pause when he finishes the last sentence of a good Lewis novel; it was the first of Lewis's books after *Free Air* to end in such a way that the reader has no doubts about the author's endorsement of the happy ending. And it is full of preciousness in word choice and rheto- ric. That Ann wants to name her unborn daughter Pride is bad enough; to describe Ann this way is worse: "She was off, a loping lioness."[5]

But as badly written as the novel is, it does provide us with some significant autobiographical insights. The way Lewis handled the relationship between Ann, the professional woman, and her seemingly less-important husband, Russell Spaulding, is suggestive of the relation- ship between Lewis and Dorothy Thompson. Spaulding is irritated in much the same manner as Lewis by the way his wife was treated as a more-important, more- engaging personality at dinner parties and other social engagements than he was. Dorothy Thompson herself sensed Lewis's resentment and indicated in a letter written to Lewis in 1932 that she was aware of the con- ceptual relationship between herself and Ann Vickers: "Sometimes I think you don't see me at all, but some- body you have made up, a piece of fiction like Ann Vickers."[6]

As difficult as it is to say anything good about *Ann Vickers,* it is even more difficult when we come to Lewis's next novel, *Work of Art,* which was published in 1934. The same criticism that Alfred Kazin leveled against *Ann Vickers* can be utilized in regard to *Work of Art.* "In some of the early brilliant descriptions . . . he seemed to be blocking out perfect scene after perfect scene that led to nothing."[7] *Work of Art* gives an inside view of the hotel industry through the story of Myron Weagle, who begins his career in the small-town hotel owned by his parents, goes up in the business, loses out through no fault of his own, and intends to start anew by turning a Kansas tourist camp into a work of art. Myron's career is contrasted with that of his supposedly more artistic brother, who aspires to be a poet and turns out to be a hack. The moral is evident enough—and that is one problem with the novel. But the descriptions of how a hotel is operated have an interest of their own, and Lewis's experience as a career-long hotel dweller is on display. The result is not very exciting, not even in a melodramatic way—something that makes its successor, Arthur Hailey's *Hotel,* a much better book. And once again Lewis ended a novel on too positive a note, abandoning the ambiguity that elevates the conclusions of his best novels.

But like *Ann Vickers, Work of Art* also contains some autobiographical implications worth noting. Myron's brother, Ora Weagle, with his adolescent poetry, has much in common with the young Sinclair Lewis. And Ora's later career, in which he writes only one memorable book, throws away much of his talent, and becomes a drunk, has at least a few parallels to Lewis's own. It is as if Lewis was exorcising his guilt at becoming a writer (instead of a physician or a "practical man," as Dr. Lewis had wished) in this depiction of Ora; and in the presentation of the business-minded Myron as the true artist, it is as if Lewis was doubting the value of his

own profession. Such doubts could only complicate
matters when the book came out because its reviewers
were hesitant to praise it; they were beginning to have
some doubts about Lewis's ability to regain his 1920s
level of achievement.

These doubts were partly laid to rest the next year
with the publication of *It Can't Happen Here,* one of
Lewis's most timely and sensational novels. *It Can't
Happen Here,* which developed out of Lewis's persistent
concern over the latent fascism in America (a concern
that can be seen in his depiction of the Good Citizens
League of *Babbitt* and the Napap of *Elmer Gantry*), is
structured around the sort of supposition Lewis the conversationalist often liked to toy with—suppose the rise to
power of a Hitler or a Mussolini had taken place in the
United States. The story line of the novel develops out
of just such a possibility. Senator Berzelius Windrip,
who was partly modeled on Huey Long, the demagogic
Louisiana politician who was assassinated shortly before
It Can't Happen Here appeared, gets elected president
by appealing to what later was to be called the Silent
Majority. Once in office, Windrip declares martial law,
rounds up the intellectuals and radicals, institutes deten-
tion camps, and establishes a corporate state. All of this
is seen from the point-of-view of Doremus Jessup, a liberal Vermont newspaper editor, who eventually turns
up in Minnesota taking part in the counterrevolution
against the Corpo regime. Since the book ends with no
definite victory in sight (though Lewis's hopes clearly
rode with Jessup), there is a return to the use of the con-
cluding ambiguity that Lewis used so well in his big
novels.

Despite the fact that it was written in only four
months, *It Can't Happen Here* did a great deal to restore
Lewis's reputation, which had been somewhat dimin-

ished by *Ann Vickers* and *Work of Art* and was not helped by the collection of his short stories that had appeared in the summer of 1935. *Selected Short Stories* sold only slightly more than 3,000 copies in hardback and revealed most of Lewis's deficiencies as a storyteller —plots that are too obviously manipulated, faulty characterization (children and girls who are too coy, men who are often either too facile or too slang-ridden in their talk), and too much willingness to please the more sentimental readers of the popular magazines. But a few of the stories, "Land" and "Young Man Axelbrod" in particular, do not share these defects and are indeed quite memorable. Nonetheless, reviewers paid the short stories scant attention—something that was certainly not true of *It Can't Happen Here,* which stirred up worldwide comment, although most readers tended to see the novel as politically, not artistically, significant.

The topicality of *It Can't Happen Here* is evident not only in the sale of 300,000 copies and its simultaneous production in thirteen cities as a Federal Theater Project play, but also in the many references to people, events, and places that were in the news in 1935. In one way or another, Lewis referred to Long's dictatorship in Louisiana, gangsterism in Chicago, the Ku Klux Klan, Father Coughlin, the modern-day forms of Tammany graft, the general acceptance of censorship, and the rabid antiintellectualism that was evident across the country. Dorothy Thompson, with her knowledge of politics and the current scene, was undoubtedly a help to Lewis in the picture he created of the Depression era. But a great deal of credit must go to Lewis himself for his attempt at regaining the sense of immediacy and the insight into the contemporary scene that he had possessed so strongly during the previous decade.

It Can't Happen Here, for all of its timeliness, is

not, however, particularly realistic. Lewis's use of caricature, his exaggerated dialogue, his rudimentary use of
plot, together with his bizarre descriptions of location,
make the novel a nightmarish thing, somewhat on the
order of *Babbitt*. Windrip's takeover and Jessup's sufferings are not presented in a believable way; but the fears
that are elicited, fears concerning the deterioration of the
human spirit in a totalitarian state, are real enough—and
it is on these fears that Lewis played. When the novel
was published, there was great uneasiness in the United
States over the rise of fascism in Europe; many Americans were actually making provisions against the day
when the same thing would happen in their own nation.
With the American economy in bad trouble and desperate men proposing desperate remedies, anxiety was
reaching the point of hysteria as the election year of 1936
approached. Lewis's novel, with its dramatization of
national fear, anxiety, and hysteria quite likely served to
release tension as well as to provide a needed warning.

It is what *It Can't Happen Here* accomplished as a
pressure valve rather than what it gave by way of solution that made it significant when it appeared. What
Lewis proposed in the novel is once again the old, although certainly vital, elevation of the critical spirit that
is endorsed in *Arrowsmith*. "I am convinced," Jessup
says near the end of the novel, "that everything that is
worth while in the world has been accomplished by the
free, inquiring, critical spirit, and that the preservation
of this spirit is more important than any social system
whatsoever."[8] Jessup is the gentleman envisioned by
Matthew Arnold, the middle-class man redeemed who
figured so prominently in Lewis's moral vision, the man
who is repelled by extremist positions of all sort, whether
put forth by the Communist Party or the D.A.R. The
right that Jessup is most willing to defend (and Lewis

along with him) is the right to lead an ordinary life. The defense of this right in the midst of the dogma delirious-ness of the 1930s, when most writers found it necessary to endorse some sort of drastic social solution, was, of course, a brave and independent thing in itself.

The threat of fascism, as many social critics have emphasized, is almost perennial in the United States, and because of this, *It Can't Happen Here* has experienced several revivals and is still in print. During the McCarthy hearings in the 1950s the novel was taken up with considerable enthusiasm, and the same thing happened during recent years as a response to the white-backlash mentality that followed the civil-rights demonstrations and campus disruptions of the 1960s.

Most readers who react enthusiastically to *It Can't Happen Here,* however, are dismayed when they come to Lewis's next novel, *The Prodigal Parents,* which ap-peared in 1938—and this would be especially true of radical students, for they are the victims of considerable critical abuse in the book. In contrast to its predecessor, *The Prodigal Parents* seems to be an illiberal, stodgy piece of writing, in which the older generation is pre-sented as the last hope for western civilization.

The story Lewis told in *The Prodigal Parents* is one that is told too seldom—the age-old revolt of children against their parents, but told from the point-of-view of the old folks. Fred Cornplow, a successful automobile dealer, and his wife have a son in college who mouths communist clichés and a daughter who is a phony radi-cal. The children turn out to be moral cowards; but the parents are more steadfast than their children and more truly free and liberal-minded—a quality of independence they demonstrate by dropping everything and leaving for Europe. At the end, Fred returns to the United States to put his son, who has become a drunk, through the cure.

Lewis missed the point of the novel's title, and this fault underscores the conceptual inadequacy of the book. The parents are not clearly seen as "prodigal" even though there is some indication that they and their generation are to be blamed for the spoiled children they have raised. But in the telling of the story, most of the blame is shifted to the younger generation, which is depicted, too simply, as no good. Lewis, of course, wrote the novel with the same audience he had had in mind while writing *Main Street;* that is, an audience composed mostly of people his own age. So it is understandable, though not excusable, that he would take the side of the older Cornplows.

Critics attacked the book for its defense of the capitalist system and the businessman. *The Prodigal Parents* certainly is a reactionary novel, especially for the 1930s when most writers felt compelled to dramatize leftist ideologies; but the critics should not have registered so much shock over what Lewis had written—he was, after all, essentially sympathetic to Babbitt and most certainly to Dodsworth. As we have seen many times before, his program of reform was directed toward the middle class; and his ideal hero was the middle-aged bourgeois, the sensible man, whether his name be Sam Dodsworth or Fred Cornplow.

As badly written as *The Prodigal Parents* is (stereotypes instead of characters, dialogue that was a little out-of-date in the 1930s, and a phony ending in which Mrs. Cornplow unexpectedly catches up with Fred and their son in the Canadian wilderness), it touches on some important matters. The 1930s was a time when communism enjoyed a mindless and faddish endorsement among the young. It was also a time when the permissive child-rearing techniques, which were emphasized during the previous decade, were being questioned. And

Lewis's satire on the absurdity of well-fed and well-dressed middle-class youth rebelling against the materialism of their parents, yet continuing to be materialistic themselves, was needed. If handled better, the novel could have been memorable—and this is the irritating thing about so many of Lewis's later books. But even so, *The Prodigal Parents* sold close to 100,000 copies.

The failure of *Bethel Merriday,* Lewis's next novel, published in 1940, was greater than that of *The Prodigal Parents,* despite the fact that it was more smoothly written. With the exception of *Bethel Merriday,* even Lewis's weakest novels are all of at least some interest because of the intellectual and social concerns that Lewis voiced in them; but *Bethel Merriday* lacks that underlying seriousness. The plot is simple enough—the account of a young actress's early career on the stage and in love. This was handled well enough to carry the reader along, but Lewis's real interest seems to have been in telling the history of a road-show production of *Romeo and Juliet* in modern dress. As much as the reader learns about trouping, the characterization suffers, and Bethel is at best an insipid heroine. Although Lewis presented a book-length consideration of whether the theater or the "real" world offers the greatest reality, the novel is nearly devoid of the relevant issues to be found in most of his books. The sales reflect the lack of interest sparked by the novel; only 30,000 copies were sold in hardcover, although book-club selection eventually led to another 50,000.

Bethel Merriday came out of Lewis's long interest in the theater and his involvement with a young actress named Marcella Powers, after whom Bethel is modeled. Lewis's theatrical inclinations extended beyond his cocktail-party mimicking of character types into playwriting and acting. In 1932 he worked on an adaptation of

Dodsworth (which later had a successful run on Broad-way); in 1935 he collaborated with Lloyd Lewis (no relation), the art critic and popular historian, on *The Jayhawkers,* a play about Civil War Kansas; and in 1938 he wrote and later starred in *Angela Is Twenty-Two,* which develops around a situation of May-December ro-mance (pointing forward to *Cass Timberlane*). Lewis also acted in Paul Vincent Carroll's *Shadow and Sub-stance,* in Thornton Wilder's *Our Town,* and in the stage version of *It Can't Happen Here* (playing the role of Doremus Jessup). Although Lewis was a capable actor, his involvement with the theater was primarily a diver-sion, a term that also applies to *Bethel Merriday* it-self.

The reviews of *Gideon Planish,* which came out in 1943, were also mainly negative, although the sale of the novel went to over 100,000 copies. Most commenta-tors, however, noticed the similarity to *Elmer Gantry* in subject matter and tone, and this similarity alone is enough to make *Gideon Planish* a considerable improve-ment over *Bethel Merriday.* With *Gideon Planish* Lewis returned to the satirical approach that accounted for much of the success he enjoyed during his greatest decade.

Gideon begins, appropriately enough, as a speech professor, marries one of his students, and gains a pushy wife. His own ambitions combined with her urgings lead him into promotional work for various foundations and agencies, among them the "Association to Promote Eskimo Culture" and the "Dynamos of Democratic Direction." Gideon has a chance to redeem himself by returning as president to the college where he began teaching, but his wife talks him out of it and he remains a flack for Colonel Marduc, the advertising tycoon. As funny as the novel often is, it suffers from too many changes of scene and too many undeveloped characters.

One of the more memorable personages in the novel, however, is Winfred Marduc Homeward, the Talking Woman, the type of lady messiah who will lecture to anyone anywhere. The Talking Woman was modeled on Dorothy Thompson, just as Fran Dodsworth was modeled on Lewis's first wife, Grace Hegger.

But *Gideon Planish* is still amusing and sometimes troubling to read today. The same aptness of description that makes *Babbitt* so engaging a book is resurrected in such descriptions as this one of the young Gideon: "a chunky young man with hair like a tortoise-shell cat."[9] And Lewis's treatment of the American obsession with red-tape foundations and oratory instead of honest action is still much to the point. But through it all is a hero who is not without some subtleties of character. Like Babbitt at the end, Gideon does realize his folly and comes to self-awareness in a way that evokes some of Lewis's old ambiguity. Has Gideon learned enough about himself or is he beyond redemption? The question, wisely, is not answered. "The distant urgent whistle of a ferry, laden with freight cars from Winnemac and Iowa and the uplands of California, awoke him, and for an instant his square face moved with smiling as in half-dreams he was certain that some day he too would take a train, and in some still valley find honor and dignity," Lewis wrote on the last page. "But the whistle sounded again, so lost and lonely that Dr. Planish fell back into his habitual doubt of himself, and his face tightened with anxiety and compromise."[10]

The problems of anxiety and compromise are handled differently in *Cass Timberlane,* published two years after *Gideon Planish* and much more of a critical and commercial success. The plot of *Cass Timberlane* points back to that of *Main Street* in its treatment of marriage. Cass Timberlane is a middle-aged judge in Grand Republic, Minnesota, a fictional city somewhat resembling

Duluth, where Lewis lived while working on part of the novel (the name Grand Republic was undoubtedly inspired by Grand Rapids, Minnesota, a city located one hundred miles northeast of Duluth). Cass courts and marries Jinny Marshland, a girl of twenty-three, who later runs off to New York with one of his friends, a cad with the caddish name of Bradd Criley. Cass eventually takes her back after rescuing her, somewhat melodramatically, from a near-fatal attack of diabetes. Lewis saw the problem of marriage as the basic one in civilization, and Cass's taking Jinny back and forgiving her is thus presented as an essential act in the reform of middle-class life in America. Cass is another of Lewis's awakened bourgeois heroes.

The novel enjoyed a large sale and it was made into a movie, starring Spencer Tracy and Lana Turner, that was one of the big box-office draws of the decade. Some male reviewers liked the book and many readers still regard it as the best novel Lewis wrote after *It Can't Happen Here*. But female reviewers generally deplored it because of the blame Lewis put on women for the horror he saw in most American marriages. This view of marriage was put forth in a bitterly satiric, although distressingly effective series of sketches entitled "An Assemblage of Husbands and Wives." As Grebstein emphasized, "these passages contain some of the best writing Lewis ever did, tight, sharp, uncluttered by specious or ambiguous emotion and sexually frank but not erotic or embarrassed. They provide counterpoint to the story of Cass and Jinny and add depth to the entire novel."[11] Lewis's attack on marriage, and women in particular, was extremely pertinent at the time. Only three years before, Philip Wylie had published his notorious *Generation of Vipers,* in which he put forth the term "momism" by way of objection to matriarchal domination in American homes.

Even though *Cass Timberlane* is one of the novels in which Lewis presented aspects of himself (the Cass-Jinny relationship has an obvious connection with Lewis's infatuation with Marcella Powers), the book never quite comes alive. The characters lack an inner existence, important questions (such as the old one Lewis asked in *Main Street* about the future of civilization in the midwest) are raised and dropped before an honest attempt is made at answering them, and the impression one gets is that Lewis lacked sufficient energy when he was writing the novel to make it succeed.

One significant development in *Cass Timberlane,* however, is that with it Lewis came back to his home country. "Lewis has returned to Minnesota to live and has written about a small Middle-Western city in a way that is quite distinct from anything in *Main Street* or *Babbitt,*" Edmund Wilson wrote in his review of the book.

These northern Middle Western cities, with their big lakes and their raw business buildings, their gloomy old houses of the eighties that run to fancy windows and towers, and their people playing bridge and drinking cocktails, kept warm by a new oil furnace, in the midst of their terrific winters, have a particular impressiveness and pathos which are sometimes rather hard to account for in terms of their constituent elements but which, despite all the crassness and dullness, are inherent in the relation of the people to the country.[12]

Lewis continued to write about Minnesota in this way through his next two novels, *Kingsblood Royal* (1947) and *The God-Seeker* (1949).

With *Kingsblood Royal* Lewis returned to the research novel in an effort that was nearly as exhaustive as that involved in the writing of *Arrowsmith*. The subject under investigation in *Kingsblood Royal* is the condition of the black man in the United States, along with the overriding consideration of race relations. Lewis's legwork included trips to the south, inspections of ghetto areas in the north, and long conversations with as many Negroes as he could get to talk to him. The results were sufficiently impressive; the novel sold over a million and a half copies and was honored by *Ebony* magazine as the book that had done the most to promote racial understanding in the year it came out.

Although many reviewers praised Lewis for the antiracist stands he took in *Kingsblood Royal,* they generally deplored the plot situation as being implausible. *Kingsblood Royal* (a name that should have been rejected before it was even put into Lewis's notebook) is a young banker in Grand Republic who learns that he has 3.125% Negro blood. He is compelled to reveal this fact and soon finds that he and his family are rejected by the Wasp social stratum of which they have been a part. The novel ends after the hero, his wife and children, and his Negro friends have unsuccessfully tried to defend themselves against an attack by a mob of vigilantes who insist that the Royals move to another neighborhood. It is difficult to believe that such a small amount of Negro blood would cause Kingsblood Royal's Minnesota neighbors so much distress. But that is not the point, and the basic situation of the novel has been almost entirely misunderstood. Lewis was saying that American attitudes toward race are so extreme that even an extremely small amount of racial difference (or difference of any sort) is likely to bring a man trouble. To Lewis, racial prejudice is another manifestation of the oppressive will toward conformity that he saw as so much a part of the American state of mind in novels like *Main Street* and *Babbitt.*

Like *It Can't Happen Here, Kingsblood Royal* must be read as a propaganda novel. Propaganda was one of

Lewis's great strengths; his ability to overstate, his tendency to concentrate on one issue so much that all else seems legitimately obscured, and his willingness to share his outrage with that of his reader all made him a superb pamphleteer. "In short, to judge *Kingsblood Royal* as a realistic novel or perhaps even as a 'satire,' in the traditional literary vein, is to judge it wrongly," Sheldon Grebstein wrote. "This is Lewis the fanatic, the crusader, the inquisitor; and the extremities in his novel are precisely those which attend crusades and inquisitions. If *Kingsblood Royal* falls short as a work of art—and we do not defend it as a work of art—it succeeds as a public service."[13]

The novel remains important in the history of the black-power movement,[14] and it is one of the few versions of black America to be written by a white man before the great civil-rights campaigns of the 1950s and 1960s and yet retain authentic touches. But its defects are nonetheless considerable. *"Kingsblood Royal* is probably one of those good bad books that, for the wrong reasons, continue to have a certain fascination," Mark Schorer suggested. "Here everything is somehow out of focus even within its own polemical perspective. The concentration on a single social problem makes an arid absurdity of the society within which it exists."[15] In addition to a tendency to make many of the characters pasteboard spokesmen for stereotyped views (the Uncle Tom, the white bigot, the back-to-Africanist, the infinitely kind-and-wise black clergyman), Lewis damaged the novel's objectivity by having too great an imbalance between the races—there are too many good blacks and too many bad whites. And it seems as if there is nothing else to talk about in Grand Republic other than the "Negro question." But then these defects are all part of the propagandist's art and are thus somewhat excusable.

One has the feeling—and it is the same feeling that most of Lewis's post-1930 novels elicit—that he should have found a better way of handling his provocative material.

The God-Seeker is a considerable departure from the type of novel that earned Lewis his reputation, the up-to-the-minute novel of controversy. *The God-Seeker,* by way of contrast, is a historical novel that opens in the 1840s. The setting is early Saint Paul, where the hero, Aaron Gadd, intends to become a missionary to the Indians but instead becomes a building contractor and gets involved in the problems of unionization. It is a partial fulfillment of the labor novel Lewis had talked about writing during the late 1920s and early 1930s. The story of Aaron Gadd was to be the first volume in a trilogy dealing with American history from the mid-nineteenth century up to the time of the writing of the novel. The novel apparently was to be followed by one on railroads (the story of James J. Hill, the Minnesota-based founder of the Great Northern, now the Burlington-Northern, Railroad), and a third, tentatively titled *Tired Warrior,* which would be the biography of an old liberal.

Lewis's projected trilogy sounds like a fascinating proposal until one reads *The God-Seeker* and realizes that Lewis's deficiencies as a historical novelist are considerable. He tended to see the nineteenth century too much in terms of the twentieth; and he was not sympathetic to the problems of earlier times, as is evident in the great contempt he displayed in *The God-Seeker* toward the Victorian missionary impulse. Lewis's lack of objectivity can also be seen, of course, in the way he attacked the narrow-mindedness of the pioneers in *Main Street,* however necessary that attack might have been in 1920.

But at least one aspect of *The God-Seeker* is impressive and of considerable relevance—the sympathetic portrayal of Indians, whose relationship with white settlers and culture is analyzed with impressive sensitivity. *The God-Seeker* treats the Indian question nearly as much and as well as *Kingsblood Royal* does the Negro question.

The novel also touches on a crucial theme in American history, a theme implied in the title. Americans seem to have been obsessed with God-seeking, from the Pilgrim Fathers on down, and Lewis attempted to dramatize this obsession in the account he gave us of Aaron Gadd's life.

However many apologies one can make for *The God-Seeker,* the weaknesses that are present in most of Lewis's novels are so obvious in it that praise must of necessity be faint. Shaky plotting, inadequate characterization, and uneven writing are but part of the difficulty; it is Lewis's tendency toward melodrama that ultimately defeats the book. The sudden rescues from blizzards become too much to take. But there is at least one thing that justifies the time Lewis spent in the Minnesota Historical Society library. "His love for his native state shines forth in *The God-Seeker,*" D. J. Dooley wrote; "he has a great deal of respect for the men who redeemed it from the wilderness,"[16] even though he provides us with little insight into why they did what they did and whether or not it was of value.

Lewis turned away from Minnesota for his last novel, *World So Wide,* which appeared posthumously. The major significance of *World So Wide,* which is set in Italy, is autobiographical, and this was discussed at length in Chapter I. But the novel represents a considerable comeback for Lewis stylistically, especially after *The God-Seeker*—something that is surprising when one considers the poor state of Lewis's health while he was writing it. Although the dialogue in *World So Wide* was criticized for being out-of-date when the book appeared in 1951, that is much less a problem in reading it now (1951 dialogue would probably sound almost as much out-of-date). The story moves along (despite being a partial repetition of the *Dodsworth* material), the style is more even than in any of Lewis's late novels, and one can conclude that *World So Wide* is a good, if not great, little novel.

The same criticism could apply to all of the novels Lewis wrote after 1930. One is often distressed at the weaknesses in them; but at the same time, *Ann Vickers* and all the rest seem surprisingly good—in places. After *Dodsworth,* with the possible exception of *World So Wide,* Lewis did not write an even book. Yet as inconsistent as he was stylistically, he still had plenty to say and a considerable number of readers who would listen. His presence was not the overwhelming thing it was during the 1920s, but he was still inescapably *there* throughout the Depression, World War II, and the coldest years of the cold war. And his voice, although less biting than it once was, remained essentially the same—the voice of the moralist, arguing and demonstrating the need for a reformed middle class.

6

The Notoriety of His Enduring Fame

For all the disorderly violence of his life he was a hard worker, and he did not give up, as many another writer has done, when it became evident that he could never again enjoy such a furor as he had once created. But he must have asked himself the question which is inevitably asked now: Had he won some enduring fame or was it all mere notoriety?

—Joseph Wood Krutch, "Sinclair Lewis,"
The Nation (24 February 1951).

Lewis's reputation has rested, and most likely will continue to rest, on his notoriety as a polemicist—and he was a good one, deserving comparison to H. L. Mencken and perhaps even to Thomas Paine. In dealing with the new realities of the American industrial state and the concurrent economy of abundance, he took a moral position that was instructive yet not so radical as to be unacceptable to the middle-class audience that bought his books. His appeal was wide, perhaps wider than that of any other American writer. He received serious critical attention from high-powered critics and scholars like Krutch and Vernon L. Parrington, yet at the same time he was read devotedly by hundreds of thousands of people whose literary acumen was anything but high-powered. He was that most unusual phenomenon, an important writer whose appeal to the masses was genuine. Lewis's big novels were not what so many highly publicized "serious" books often turn out to be—items for the coffee table. They were read, and the arguments they presented were issues for conversation all over the country, as if Lewis were in the center of a nation-wide dialogue. But as much as Lewis deserves credit as an author of books that have been seen as publishing events and as markers in the history of American consciousness, he is nonetheless a novelist, and his place in the history of that literary form is a definite one.

The novel is, of course, many things, and the Lewis novel is a distinct type, never matched or really imitated by any other writer, however many bad or weak novels Lewis wrote. Although Lewis's presence was most certainly felt by other writers, he did not, in the strictest sense at any rate, inspire a school of followers: one reason for this is that his most memorable books are all *tours de force,* making imitation difficult. But a more sweeping explanation is that there is a quality of inimitableness in Lewis; as has been suggested in an earlier chapter, he is virtually a movement unto himself. He is not literally a realist. Naturalism is not quite an appropriate word to use in describing his approach. He was not a member of the Lost Generation. And even in Mencken's circle he was more than a little out of place. To be certain, a good writer must be beyond the possibilities of rigid classification, but as a review of Lewis's background readily indicates, he has been more difficult to place in perspective than most.

The problem of understanding Lewis has not simply been a matter of evaluating his social pronouncements or of debating whether or not he is sufficiently artistic; it has been predominately the problem of his uniqueness. There is a wildness, an unpredictableness that is at the center of Lewis the man and Lewis the writer; and this tendency at once serves as an explanation for the dynamism of his writing and the inertia that has crept into many of the attempts to evaluate it. One is led to conclude that the nervous energy that is so much a part of Lewis's style, tends to wear readers and critics down; defeats them just as Lewis's presence at a cocktail party often exhausted the other guests. There is no point in explaining away this characteristic of the Lewis novel other than to state simply that Lewis is no writer to read in large doses; he is too singular, too angry, too irritating in both style and statement. This, of course, is a major source of his power, a way he still makes the presence of his abrasive personality felt.

If there is a single word that may be used to describe and categorize Lewis's books, it is none of the adjectives so far mentioned. The best term is perhaps "garish." His better novels are all showy, harsh, glaring, and alternately positive or negative to the point of extravagance. They embody a particular kind of contemporaneity that is effectively defined in the word "pop" and its implication of obsession with the bizarre forms and life patterns that are part of the everyday world in the economy-of-abundance democracies of this century. In many respects Lewis was the first of our pop novelists (later ones include Dos Passos, Gore Vidal, Terry Southern, and the Charles Portis of *Norwood*), his imagination seemingly most stirred by the ticky-tacky eternal presence of mass culture seen on the big screen at the Rosebud Theater, listened to on the radio, tasted through a soda-shop straw, touched with gloves purchased at the Bon Ton store, and smelled through a miasma of automobile exhaust and industrial smoke. It is a culture in which the ultimate disillusionment is that in the midst of seemingly infinite variety so many things are the same and carry the same price tag—loss of freedom. But Lewis reveled in it nonetheless, inexplicably loving that which he invited us to hate.

But the nature of the Lewis novel and the reasons for his popularity should first and last be understood in ways that do not demand footnotes in the history of aesthetics. Lewis came on the scene at just the moment when twentieth-century American garishness was becoming apparent—even to Americans. It was a time when the very garishness of the reality of surplus production was short-circuiting the pioneer brain. His novels are partly histories of the painful transition that began sometime around 1920 and partly remedies for the pain. His fictionalizing of what was happening in the small town and in the city to the housewife, the businessman, the scientist, the preacher, and the industrialist was a purgation of fears that were widely and deeply felt, fears that are, of course, still with us. Had Lewis's novels not been written the way they were, had they been more tightly structured, more carefully thought-out, more Jamesian (for it is Henry James that most critics seem to have in mind when castigating Lewis), they would not have had the peculiar and lasting effect that they have. This itself is a measure of Lewis's artistry and a defense of his achievement as a writer, of the notoriety of his enduring fame.

Notes

1. The Exaggerated Melodrama

1. Frederick F. Manfred, "Sinclair Lewis: A Portrait," *American Scholar* 23 (1954):165.
2. Vincent Sheean, *Dorothy and Red* (Boston, 1963), p. 344.
3. *New Republic* 21 (28 January 1920):275.
4. George H. Douglas, "Main Street after Fifty Years," *Prairie Schooner* 44 (Winter 1970–71):343.
5. Frederick F. Manfred and James Lundquist, "Frederick Manfred Talks about Sinclair Lewis," *Sinclair Lewis Newsletter* 2 (1970):2.
6. James J. Napier, "Letters of Sinclair Lewis to Joseph Hergesheimer, 1915–22," *American Literature* 38 (1966):237.
7. Norman Mailer, *Advertisements for Myself,* Berkley edition (New York, 1966), p. 85.
8. Sinclair Lewis, "Minnesota, the Norse State," in *The Man from Main Street,* eds. Harry E. Maule and Melville H. Cane (New York, 1953), p. 274.
9. E. M. Forster, "Our Photography: Sinclair Lewis," in *Sinclair Lewis: A Collection of Critical Essays,* ed. Mark Schorer (Englewood Cliffs, N. J., 1962), p. 95.
10. Sinclair Lewis, *Main Street,* Signet Classic edition (New York, 1961), p. 28.

11. Lewis, *Main Street,* p. 29.

12. Sinclair Lewis, "The Long Arm of the Small Town," in *The Man from Main Street,* p. 272.

13. Lewis, "Minnesota, the Norse State," p. 283.

14. Ibid.

15. H. L. Mencken, "Portrait of an American Citizen," in *Sinclair Lewis: A Collection of Critical Essays,* p. 22.

16. Vernon L. Parrington, "Sinclair Lewis: Our Own Diogenes," in *Sinclair Lewis: A Collection of Critical Essays,* pp. 64–65.

17. Sinclair Lewis, "How I Wrote a Novel on Trains and beside the Kitchen Sink," in *The Man from Main Street,* p. 203.

18. Napier, "Letters of Sinclair Lewis to Joseph Hergesheimer," pp. 245–46.

19. Grace Hegger Lewis, *With Love from Gracie: Sinclair Lewis 1912–1925* (New York, 1955), p. 134.

20. Sheean, *Dorothy and Red,* p. 146.

21. Carl Bode, *Mencken* (Carbondale, Indiana, 1969), p. 173.

22. Grace Hegger Lewis, *With Love from Gracie,* p. 207.

23. Sheean, *Dorothy and Red,* p. 8.

24. Dale Warren, "Notes on a Genius: Sinclair Lewis at His Best," *Harpers* 208 (January 1954):62.

25. Grace Hegger Lewis, *With Love from Gracie,* p. 79.

26. Ibid., p. 112.

27. Ibid., p. 10.

28. Sheean, *Dorothy and Red,* p. 177.

29. Mark Schorer, *Sinclair Lewis: An American Life* (New York, 1961), p. 57.

30. Manfred, "Sinclair Lewis: A Portrait," p. 183.

31. Sheean, *Dorothy and Red,* p. 297.

32. Manfred, "Sinclair Lewis: A Portrait," p. 173.

33. Charles Breasted, "The Sauk-Centricities of Sinclair Lewis," *Saturday Review of Literature* 37 (14 August 1954):8.

34. Sinclair Lewis, *World So Wide,* Pyramid edition (New York, 1961), p. 26.

35.' Ibid., p. 27.
36. Ibid., p. 28.
37. Ibid., p. 12.
38. Ibid., p. 189.

2. *"Moralities for a New Time"*

1. William E. Leuchtenburg, *The Perils of Prosperity* (Chicago, 1958), p. 11.
2. Alfred Kazin, *On Native Grounds* (Garden City, N.Y., 1956), p. 180.
3. Sinclair Lewis, *The Man Who Knew Coolidge* (New York, 1928), p. 254.
4. Sinclair Lewis, "The Passing of Capitalism," in *The Man from Main Street,* eds. Harry E. Maule and Melville H. Cane (New York, 1953), p. 328.
5. Sinclair Lewis, *Main Street,* Signet Classics edition (New York, 1961), p. 134.
6. Ibid., p. 134.
7. Ibid., p. 149.
8. Ibid., p. 60.
9. Ibid., pp. 7–8.
10. Ibid., p. 403.
11. Cited in *This Fabulous Century,* 1910–1920, Time-Life Books (New York, 1969), p. 23.
12. Sinclair Lewis, *Babbitt,* Signet Classics edition (New York, 1961), pp. 189–90.
13. Ibid., p. 277.
14. Ibid., p. 152.
15. Ibid., p. 53.
16. Ibid., p. 55.
17. Mark Schorer, *Sinclair Lewis: An American Life* (New York, 1961), p. 438.
18. D. J. Dooley, *The Art of Sinclair Lewis* (Lincoln, Neb., 1967), p. 118.
19. Sheldon Norman Grebstein, *Sinclair Lewis* (New York, 1962), p. 98.

20. Lewis, *Babbitt,* p. 123.
21. Sinclair Lewis, *Mantrap* (New York, 1926), p. 56.
22. Ibid.
23. Sinclair Lewis, *Elmer Gantry,* Signet Classics edition (New York, 1967), p. 34.
24. Ibid., p. 394.
25. Ibid., p. 416.
26. Lewis, *The Man Who Knew Coolidge,* p. 261.
27. Ibid., p. 262.
28. Sinclair Lewis, *Dodsworth,* Signet Classics edition (New York, 1967), p. 22.
29. Ibid.
30. Stephen S. Conroy, "Sinclair Lewis's Sociological Imagination," *American Literature* 42 (November 1970):360.
31. Walter Lippmann, "Sinclair Lewis," in *Sinclair Lewis: A Collection of Critical Essays,* ed. Mark Schorer (Englewood Cliffs, N. J., 1962), p. 84.

3. The Question of Art

1. Mark Schorer, *Sinclair Lewis: An American Life* (New York, 1961), p. 813.
2. H. L. Mencken, "Consolation," in *Sinclair Lewis: A Collection of Critical Essays,* ed. Mark Schorer (Englewood Cliffs, N. J., 1962), p. 19.
3. Sherwood Anderson, "Sinclair Lewis," in *Sinclair Lewis: A Collection of Critical Essays,* p. 27.
4. T. K. Whipple, "Sinclair Lewis," in *Sinclair Lewis: A Collection of Critical Essays,* p. 71.
5. Robert Cantwell, "Sinclair Lewis," in *Sinclair Lewis: A Collection of Critical Essays,* p. 111.
6. Sinclair Lewis, *Main Street,* Signet Classics edition (New York, 1961), p. 305.
7. Ibid., p. 407.
8. Ibid., p. 7.

9. Sinclair Lewis, *Babbitt,* Signet Classics edition (New York, 1961), p. 87.

10. Rebecca West, "Sinclair Lewis Introduces Elmer Gantry," in *Sinclair Lewis: A Collection of Critical Essays,* p. 39.

11. Sinclair Lewis, *World So Wide,* Pyramid edition (New York, 1961), pp. 96–97.

12. Sinclair Lewis, "A Letter on Style," in *The Man from Main Street,* eds. Harry E. Maule and Melville H. Cane (New York, 1953), p. 189.

13. Sheldon Norman Grebstein, *Sinclair Lewis* (New York, 1962), p. 20.

14. Lewis, *Main Street,* p. 243.

15. Ibid., p. 23.

16. Ibid., p. 417.

17. Lewis, *Babbitt,* p. 220.

18. Maxwell Geismer, *Last of the Provincials* (Boston, 1947), p. 97.

19. Lewis, *Babbitt,* p. 6.

20. Ibid., p. 309.

21. Ibid.

22. Ibid., p. 316.

23. Joseph Wood Krutch, "Mr. Babbitt's Spiritual Guide," in *Sinclair Lewis: A Collection of Critical Essays,* p. 38.

24. Sinclair Lewis, *Elmer Gantry,* Signet Classics edition (New York, 1967), p. 14.

25. Constance Rourke, "Round Up," in *Sinclair Lewis: A Collection of Critical Essays,* p. 29.

26. Lewis, *Gantry,* p. 416.

27. *From Main Street to Stockholm: Letters of Sinclair Lewis, 1919–1930,* ed. Harrison Smith (New York, 1952), p. 229.

28. Sinclair Lewis, *The Man Who Knew Coolidge* (New York, 1928), p. 174.

29. Grebstein, *Sinclair Lewis,* p. 113.

30. Robert L. Coard, "Dodsworth and the Question of Art," *Sinclair Lewis Newsletter* 3 (1971).

31. Grace Hegger Lewis, *With Love From Gracie: Sinclair Lewis, 1912–1925* (New York, 1955), p. 187.

4. *The Essayist*

1. Sinclair Lewis, "Self-Conscious America," *American Mercury* 6 (October 1925):130

2. Ibid., p. 133.

3. Ibid., p. 135.

4. Sinclair Lewis, "Can an Artist Live in America?" *Nation* 121 (9 December 1925):663

5. Sinclair Lewis, "The American Fear of Literature," in *The Man from Main Street*, eds. Harry E. Maule and Melville H. Cane (New York, 1953), p. 16.

6. Ibid., p. 10.

7. Ibid., pp. 6–7.

8. Ibid., p. 12.

9. Ibid., p. 17.

10. Review of Henry S. Canby's *Age of Confidence*, in *Saturday Review of Literature* 11 (6 October 1934): 157.

11. Ibid., p. 157.

12. Sinclair Lewis, "Literary Felonies," *Saturday Review of Literature* 14 (3 October 1935):3.

13. Lewis, "Self-Conscious America," p. 131.

14. Lewis, "My First Day in New York," in *The Man from Main Street*, p. 59.

15. Lewis, "Two Yale Men in Utopia," in *The Man from Main Street,* p. 63.

16. Lewis, "I'm an Old Newspaperman Myself," in *The Man from Main Street*, p. 76.

17. Ibid., p. 89.

18. Ibid., p. 88.

19. Ibid., p. 95.

20. Lewis, "The Death of Arrowsmith," in *The Man from Main Street*, pp. 104–105.

21. Ibid., p. 106.

22. Ibid.
23. Lewis, "This Golden Half-Century, 1885–1935," in
    The Man from Main Street, p. 268.

5. *The Survivor*

1. Sinclair Lewis, "Self-Portrait," in *The Man from
   Main Street*, eds. Harry E. Maule and Melville H.
   Cane (New York, 1953), p. 55.
2. Ibid., p. 54.
3. Mark Schorer, *Sinclair Lewis: An American Life*
   (New York, 1961), p. 581.
4. Sinclair Lewis, *Ann Vickers* (Garden City, 1933),
   p. 305.
5. Ibid., p. 80.
6. Schorer, *Sinclair Lewis*, p. 576.
7. Alfred Kazin, *On Native Grounds* (Garden City,
   N. Y., 1956), p. 179.
8. Sinclair Lewis, *It Can't Happen Here* (Garden City,
   N. Y., 1935), p. 433.
9. Sinclair Lewis, *Gideon Planish* (New York, 1943),
   p. 4.
10. Ibid., p. 438.
11. Sheldon Norman Grebstein, *Sinclair Lewis* (New
    York, 1962), pp. 150–51.
12. Edmund Wilson, "Salute to an Old Landmark: Sin-
    clair Lewis," in *Sinclair Lewis: A Collection of Criti-
    cal Essays*, ed. Mark Schorer (Englewood Cliffs, N. J.,
    1962), p. 140.
13. Grebstein, *Sinclair Lewis*, p. 155.
14. *See* Lawrence Ianni, "Sinclair Lewis as a Prophet of
    Black Pride," *Sinclair Lewis Newsletter* 3 (1971):
    13–15, 21.
15. Schorer, *Sinclair Lewis*, p. 759.
16. D. J. Dooley, *The Art of Sinclair Lewis* (Lincoln,
    1967), p. 230.

Bibliography

1. Works by Sinclair Lewis

NOVELS

Hike and the Aeroplane. (Published under the pseudonym "Tom Graham.") New York: Stokes, 1912.

Our Mr. Wrenn. New York: Harper, 1914.

The Trail of the Hawk. New York: Harper, 1915.

The Job. New York: Harper, 1917.

The Innocents. New York: Harper, 1917.

Free Air. New York: Harcourt, Brace and Howe, 1919.

Main Street. New York: Harcourt, Brace, 1920.

Babbitt. New York: Harcourt, Brace, 1922.

Arrowsmith. New York: Harcourt, Brace, 1925.

Mantrap. New York: Harcourt, Brace, 1926.

Elmer Gantry. New York: Harcourt, Brace, 1927.

The Man Who Knew Coolidge. New York: Harcourt, Brace, 1928.

Dodsworth. New York: Harcourt, Brace, 1929.

Ann Vickers. Garden City: Doubleday, Doran, 1933.

Work of Art. Garden City: Doubleday, Doran, 1934.

It Can't Happen Here. Garden City: Doubleday, Doran, 1935.

The Prodigal Parents. Garden City: Doubleday, Doran, 1938.

Bethel Merriday. Garden City: Doubleday, Doran, 1940.

Gideon Planish. New York: Random House, 1943.

Cass Timberlane. New York: Random House, 1945.

Kinsgblood Royal. New York: Random House, 1947.

The God-Seeker. New York: Random House, 1949.

World So Wide. New York: Random House, 1951.

SHORT STORIES

Selected Short Stories. Garden City: Doubleday, Doran, 1935.

I'm a Stranger Here Myself, and Other Stories. Selected, with an introduction by Mark Schorer. New York: Dell, 1962.

PLAYS

Jayhawker. In collaboration with Lloyd Lewis. Garden City: Doubleday, Doran, 1935.

It Can't Happen Here, A New Version. New York: Dramatists Play Service, 1938.

Storm in the West. In collaboration with Dore Schary. (Screenplay.) New York: Stein and Day, 1963.

ESSAYS

The Man from Main Street. Edited by Harry E. Maule and Melville H. Cane. New York: Random House, 1953.

LETTERS

From Main Street to Stockholm: Letters of Sinclair Lewis, 1919–1930. Selected and with an introduction by Harrison Smith. New York: Harcourt, Brace, 1952.

Napier, James J. "Letters of Sinclair Lewis to Joseph Her-
    gesheimer, 1915–1922." *American Literature* 38
    (1966):236–46.

2. *Works about Sinclair Lewis*

BIBLIOGRAPHY

Lundquist, James. *Checklist of Sinclair Lewis.* Columbus:
    Charles E. Merrill, 1970.

BIOGRAPHIES

Lewis, Grace Hegger. *With Love from Gracie: Sinclair
    Lewis, 1912–1925.* New York: Harcourt, Brace, 1955.
Schorer, Mark. *Sinclair Lewis: An American Life.* New
    York: McGraw Hill, 1961.
Sheean, Vincent. *Dorothy and Red.* Boston: Houghton
    Mifflin, 1963.

SHORT GENERAL INTRODUCTIONS

Dooley, D. J. *The Art of Sinclair Lewis.* Lincoln: Uni-
    versity of Nebraska Press, 1967.
Grebstein, Sheldon Norman. *Sinclair Lewis.* New York:
    Twayne, 1962.
Schorer, Mark. *Sinclair Lewis.* University of Minnesota
    Pamphlets on American Writers, No. 27. Minneapolis:
    University of Minnesota Press, 1963.

INTERPRETATIONS OF LEWIS'S MAIN WORKS

Main Street
Herron, Ima H. *The Small Town in American Literature,*
    pp. 377–90. Durham: Duke University Press, 1939.

Hilfer, Anthony Channell. *The Revolt from the Village,*
    pp. 158–92. Chapel Hill: University of North Caro-
    lina Press, 1969.

Babbitt
Light, Martin, ed. *Studies in Babbitt.* Columbus: Charles E.
    Merrill, 1971.

Arrowsmith
Griffin, Robert J., ed. *Twentieth Century Interpretations of
    Arrowsmith: A Collection of Critical Essays.* Engle-
    wood Cliffs: Prentice-Hall, 1968.

Elmer Gantry
Moore, James B. "The Sources of *Elmer Gantry.*" *New Re-
    public* 143 (8 August 1960): 17–18.
Schorer, Mark. "The Monstrous Self-Deception of Elmer
    Gantry." *New Republic* 133 (31 October 1955): 13–
    15.

Dodsworth
Brown, Daniel R. "The Cosmopolitan Novel: James and
    Lewis." *Sinclair Lewis Newsletter* 1 (1969):6–9.
Coard, Robert L. "*Dodsworth* and the Question of Art."
    Sinclair Lewis Newsletter 3 (1971):16–18.

OTHER BIOGRAPHICAL WORKS OF SPECIAL INTEREST

Austin, Allen. "An Interview with Sinclair Lewis." *Uni-
    versity of Kansas City Review* 24 (1958):199–210.
Derleth, August. "Three Literary Men: A Memoir of Sin-
    clair Lewis, Sherwood Anderson, and Edgar Lee
    Masters." *Arts in Society,* Winter 1959, pp. 11–46.
Lewis, Claude. *Treaty Trip.* Edited by Donald Greene and
    George Knox. Minneapolis: University of Minnesota
    Press, 1959.

Manfred, Frederick F. "Sinclair Lewis: A Portrait." *American Scholar* 23 (1954):162–84.

Nathan, George Jean. "Memories of Fitzgerald, Lewis and Dreiser." *Esquire* 50 (October 1958):148–54.

Schulberg, Budd. "Lewis: Big Wind from Sauk Centre." *Esquire* 54 (1961):110–14.

Thompson, Dorothy. "The Boy and Man from Sauk Centre." *Atlantic* 206 (November 1960):39–48.

CRITICAL WORKS OF SPECIAL INTEREST

Babcock, C. Merton. "Americanisms in the Novels of Sinclair Lewis." *American Speech* 35 (May 1960):110–16.

Brown, Deming. "Sinclair Lewis: The Russian View." *American Literature* 25 (March 1953):1–12.

Bucco, Martin, "The Serialized Novels of Sinclair Lewis." *Western American Literature* 4 (1969):29–37.

Coard, Robert L. "Names in the Fiction of Sinclair Lewis." *Georgia Review* 16 (1962):318–29.

Davis, Jack L. "Mark Schorer's Sinclair Lewis." *Sinclair Lewis Newsletter* 3 (1971):3–9.

Flanagan, John T. "The Minnesota Backgrounds of Sinclair Lewis's Fiction." *Minnesota History* 37 (March 1960):1–13.

Fleissner, Robert F. "Charles Dickens and Sinclair Lewis: An Exordium." *Sinclair Lewis Newsletter* 3 (1971):10–13.

Ianni, Lawrence. "Sinclair Lewis as a Prophet of Black Pride." *Sinclair Lewis Newsletter* 3 (1971):13–15, 21.

Light, Martin. "H. G. Wells and Sinclair Lewis: Friendship, Literary Influence, and Letters." *English Fiction in Transition (1880–1920)* 5 (1962):1–20.

Lundquist, James. "Acceptance and Assent." *Sinclair Lewis Newsletter* 1 (1969):1.

————. "*World So Wide* and Sinclair Lewis's Rewritten Life." *Sinclair Lewis Newsletter* 2 (1970):12–14.

Petrullo, Helen B. "*Babbitt* as Situational Satire." *Kansas Quarterly* 1 (1969):89–97.

Index

148 *Index*